D1460087

THE LITTLE BOOK OF
PORSCHE

Written by Philip Raby

THE LITTLE BOOK OF
PORSCHE

This edition first published in the UK in 2005
By Green Umbrella

© Green Umbrella Publishing 2006

www.greenumbrella.co.uk

Publishers Jules Gammond, Tim Exell, Vanessa Gardner

Printed and bound in China

ISBN 1-905009-33-X

The views in this book are those of the author but they are general views
only and readers are urged to consult the relevant and qualified specialist
for individual advice in particular situations.

Green Umbrella Sport and Leisure hereby exclude all liability to the
extent permitted by law of any errors or omissions in this book and for
any loss, damage or expense (whether direct or indirect) suffered by a
third party relying on any information contained in this book.

All our best endeavours have been made to secure copyright clearance
for every photograph used but in the event of any copyright owner being
overlooked please address correspondence to Green Umbrella Publishing,
Suite 7, Heritage House, Eastcott Corner, Bath Road, Swindon SN1 3LS

Contents

4 – 53   A brief history of Porsche

54 – 75   Porsche in Motorsport

76 – 115   Porsches through the years

116 – 125   Things you didn't know about Porsche

PORSCHE

Chapter 1

A brief history of Porsche

Ferdinand Porsche

THE STORY OF PORSCHE BEGAN with a remarkable man – Ferdinand Porsche, who was born on 3rd September 1875 in Maffersdorf, which is now part of the Czech Republic. Despite not excelling at school, the young Ferdinand was fascinated by all things mechanical and electrical, and even produced a generator for his family's home, much to his father's chagrin. Mr Porsche senior wanted his son to follow in his own footsteps and work for the family metal-working business, but

Ferdinand had greater ambitions and got himself a job in Vienna, at a company called Bela Egger. He began as a labourer, but soon worked his way up to a management position.

During his four years in Vienna, the young Porsche was desperate to further his education, but lacked sufficient funds to pay for college, so he sneaked into classes at the Technical University to learn whatever he could about engineering and electrics. He also met his future wife, Aloisia, who worked in the same office as Ferdinand.

Porsche's enthusiasm for the exciting new science of electricity soon brought

4 | THE LITTLE BOOK OF PORSCHE

A BRIEF HISTORY OF PORSCHE

individual electric motors drove the front wheels, thereby eliminating the need for any form of traditional drivetrain, thus saving weight and making the car more efficient. Unfortunately, this weight saving was lost by the need for big and heavy batteries and so the car's performance and range were limited.

Nonetheless, Ferdinand was encouraged by the positive feedback his creation received, and he went on to develop the concept further. Later Lohner-Porsches, as they became known, were developed for racing and so became lighter and faster. Porsche even experimented with four-wheel-drive by fitting a motor to each wheel. There was also a hybrid version that used a gas power to generate electricity for the motors. Today, it's astonishing just how ahead of their time Ferdinand's concepts were – front-wheel-drive, four-wheel-drive, electric power, hybrid power were all unheard

him to the attention of Jacob Lohner, a Vienna coachbuilder who believed electric cars were the future. Lohner took on Ferdinand as an engineer and test-driver and set him to work developing an electric-powered car.

Two years later, the first Porsche-designed vehicle was displayed at the Paris Exposition of 1900, where it created quite a stir. The 25-year-old had come up with a unique design whereby

A BRIEF HISTORY OF PORSCHE

utation as a talented engineer and, in 1905, he became a Technical Director at Austro-Daimler, a branch of the German Daimler company and the largest car maker in Austria. Here, the 31-year-old developed more conventional cars, although he also designed a streamlined machine to compete in the Prince Henry Trials, a speed and reliability content that was hotly contested throughout Europe. Porsche dismissed the massive 20-litre engines of his competitors and opted instead for a 5.4-litre four-cylinder engine that produced 95bhp. In a lightweight bodyshell, this propelled the car to 90mph and ensured victory in the top three places for Austro-Daimler.

Significantly, during these early years Ferdinand worked on other pet projects, including a four-cylinder, horizontally opposed aircraft engine, that bore similarities with the Volkswagen engine that would follow.

During the First World War, Ferdinand Porsche continued to work for Austro-Daimler, which by this time had taken control of the armament

of in the early 20th century and, indeed, car manufacturers are still struggling to adopt some of the ideas one hundred years on.

The Lohner-Porsches may not have been a commercial success, but they helped Ferdinand Porsche to gain a rep-

company, Skoda. Porsche developed electric-powered trailers for transporting massive 26-ton cannons over difficult terrain. In 1916 he was awarded an honorary doctorate by the Vienna Technical University – the very establishment he'd sneaked into as a teenager.

After the war ended, Porsche became Managing Director of Austro-Daimler

and was faced with the formidable task of rebuilding the company. The local economy was in a bad way and Ferdinand believed that the large cars that his factory used to build were no longer viable, and small, efficient cars were required. However, he was unable to persuade his board that this was the way to travel. Instead, he became

BELOW Ferdinand Porsche at the wheel of an Austro-Daimler Tulpenwagen

involved in the design of a lightweight racing car called the Sascha. This had a tiny four-cylinder 1100cc engine and won its class at the 1922 Targa Floria road race.

ABOVE Ferdinand behind the wheel of one of his creations

Frustrated with Austro-Daimler, Porsche resigned in 1922 and moved to Stuttgart in Germany, where he became Chief Designer at Daimler, taking over from Paul Daimler, the founder's son.

Here Ferdinand was involved in the design and development of racing cars, in particular the small 2.0-litre super-charged machines which he made reliable and successful; one won the 1924 Targa Florio.

In 1926 Daimler merged with Mercedes and Porsche found himself involved in quite different cars, namely the large Mercedes-Benz K and S series saloons. Fitted with Porsche-designed six-cylinder, supercharged engines, these powerful beasts had some success in racing guise, but were a long way from the affordable car that Ferdinand had long dreamt of. In 1928 he resigned from Daimler Benz after his proposals for an affordable Daimler were turned down.

Porsche and his family then returned to Austria where he worked for a year at Steyr. Here he developed a 2.0-litre, six-cylinder car with independent suspension, and a larger 5.3-litre eight-cylinder version. Both cars were favourably received but in 1929 the company ran into financial difficulties and was taken over by Austro-Daimler. Not wanting to work for that firm again, Porsche resigned and, at the age of 55, was unemployed.

Dr. Ing. H.c. F. Porsche GmbH

DESPITE RECEIVING OFFERS OF work from Skoda and General Motors, Ferdinand Porsche decided it was time to set up his own business – he'd had enough of the bureaucracy of large companies. He returned to Stuttgart in 1930 and called his new design consultancy *Dr. Ing. H.c. F. Porsche GmbH, Konstruktionsbüro für Motoren Fahreug, Luftfahrzueg, und Wasserfahrzeugbau* – designers of motors, automobiles, aeroplanes and ships. An impressive list!

Ferdinand took on a staff of talented engineers, including his 21-year-old son (also called Ferdinand, but known as Ferry) who had inherited his father's skills as an engineer and designer. Porsche Junior had taken an interest in cars from an early age, and spent all his spare time at his father's place of work, asking probing questions of the staff. Also employed was Dr Anton Piëch, Ferdinand Porsche's son-in-law.

The fledgling company's first commission was to design a small saloon car for the Wanderer company. This was significant because it marked the start of Porsche's sequential numbering system for its projects – Ferdinand felt it prudent to start with the number seven, so as not to make it obvious the company was new. This was followed by Project 8, a larger, eight-cylinder car for

BELOW Ferdinand Porsche Snr (right), with his son 'Ferry' looking on, 1955

A BRIEF HISTORY OF PORSCHE

Wanderer. Sadly, the Wanderer company was taken over by Auto Union and the project was scrapped, although Ferdinand Porsche used the streamlined prototype as his personal transport for the next four years.

Business was then slack, so Ferdinand used the time to progress his plans for a small, affordable car – something his staff did at first not share his enthusiasm for. Then Zündapp, a motorcycle manufacturer, asked Porsche to design a *Volksauto* – people's car. This streamlined car became Project 12 and featured a rear-mounted five-cylinder, water-cooled radial engine. Unfortunately, Zündapp cancelled the commission partway through. However, soon after, NSU asked Porsche to design something similar. This was called Type 32 and had an air-cooled, rear-mounted engine and revolutionary torsion-bar suspension. Again, though the project was cancelled.

In 1932, Ferdinand Porsche was approached by the Russian Government and asked to become their State Designer. However, he felt that, at the age of 60, he was too old to move to a foreign country where he didn't know the language and, beside, the Russians were not interested in his 'peoples' car'.

Business was tough for Porsche's company until 1933 when Adolf Hitler announced that cars and motorcycles would no longer be taxed and that a new network of *autobahns* would be built across Germany. What's more, the government would sponsor the building of Grand Prix cars to help promote German superiority. Ferdinand Porsche got the 500,000 Mark contract to develop these racing cars, in conjunction with Auto Union. The resulting Auto Union P-Wagon was way ahead of its time with a mid-mounted V16 engine and streamlined body. The car was a success but Hitler also called for a 'volks wagen' (peoples' car) that could be sold for under 1000 Marks. At this low price, the car manufacturers said it couldn't be done, but Ferdinand Porsche met with Hitler to discuss the

proposal, and was asked to come up with a prototype.

Luckily, Porsche could draw on the work he'd done for Zündapp and NSU, and so it wasn't difficult to build three prototypes of Type 60 in 1936. With its horizontally opposed flat-four engine mounted at the rear and distinctive streamlined bodywork, this was approved by the government and a further 30 prototypes were built by Daimler-Benz in 1937. These VW30 cars were tested over more than a million miles by German troops and the following year, work started on a new factory near Wolfsburg in Saxony. The plan was that people would collect saving stamps to buy the 990 Mark car.

ABOVE Hitler seems amused that the engine is in back, as Ferdinand Snr demonstrates

However, the Second World War put paid to this idea, and the factory was used to produce military vehicles-from 1940.

Ferdinand Porsche were drawn into the war effort and spent much of his time at Wolfsburg designing tanks and a military version of the Volkswagen

BELOW 356 displayed at the 36th International Motor Exhibition, 1951

called the *Kübelwagen* or bucket car. However, he still found time to indulge his own ideas, including the Type 60K10 sports car that he'd built in 1939. Based on Volkswagen underpinnings, this streamlined car hinted at the shape of Porsches to be.

When the war ended, the Wolfsburg factory was taken over by allied troops and Ferdinand Porsche and his colleague Anton Piëch were imprisoned in France, charged with being war criminals. After 20 months' incarceration, they were released in 1947, after the Porsche family paid a bail of 500,000 Francs for each of the men – money that Ferry Porsche had earned by designing the Type 360 Cisitalia racing car.

The first Porsche

FERRY HAD ALSO BEEN DABBLING with a news sports car that used modified Volkswagen parts clothed in a sleek bodyshell. His father liked what he saw and Project 356 was progressed. Working in an old wooden sawmill in

the Austrian town of Gmünd, a small team struggled with poor parts supply to produce 356/001 – the first ever Porsche-proper. Mechanically, this was near-identical to a Volkswagen, with torsion-bar suspension, drum brakes and a 1131cc flat-four, water-cooled engine that produced 40bhp. However, the big difference was that the engine was mid-mounted in front of the transaxle, to give better weight distribution. There was a lightweight tubular

spaceframe chassis, too, and on this was mounted a smooth and elegant open-top bodyshell.

The team then made a decision that would have an impact on the designs of future Porsches – they decided to scrap the mid-engined layout because it took up too much interior space and, instead, mount the engine at the rear, like a Volkswagen. At the same time, the expensive spaceframe chassis was scrapped in favour of a Volkswagen-like

ABOVE 356 Speedster, 1955

welded steel box-section design. A second prototype, 356/002, was built, using hand-formed aluminium and steel body panels and, this time, a close coupe roof. The engine was still the same Volkswagen unit, uprated to give 40bhp, but in the streamlined body it gave a top speed of 88mph, while returning 30mph.

This prototype generated a lot of interest and Porsche soon received its first order; a Swiss dealer asked for four cars. Between 1948 and 1951, Porsche hand-built 50 356s – all slightly different – at the Gmünd workshop, with coachbuilder Beutler making a further five Cabriolets with a slightly different body shape.

The new Porsche car was a success and it was clear that the cottage industry style of production would have to change to meet demand. A decision was made to relocate to Stuttgart in Germany, where Porsche's old facility had become available again. At the same time, the 356 was 'productionised'. It looked the same, but now had an all-steel body, instead of part-aluminium. This was done to save money and because steel was easier to form and to weld. The car was also give a slightly higher roof and bonnet, and more curved sides, to increase interior space.

The engine remained Volkswagen-based but Porsche developed it to produce more power and mated it to a Getrag gearbox with synchromesh on all four forward gears. Between 1950 and 1955, Porsche sold no less than 10,000 of this first production 356 – which is now known as the 'Pre A'. Many of the cars were exported to the USA, from 1950, while the UK received right-hand-drive examples from 1951.

The 356 continued to evolve over the years until the early 1960s, when it was superseded by the larger and more powerful 911. It was fitted with larger and more powerful engines, the body shape evolved and there were various special versions. The most famous being the Speedsters, which featured chopped-down windscreens and a low hood to give an ultra-sleek look.

During its lifetime the 356 confirmed Porsche's position as a manufacturer of performance cars. Sadly, though, Ferdinand Porsche Senior died in January 1951 before the car really took off, and so he never really saw his dream realised.

BELOW 356A 1600, 1958

ABOVE 911 Targa 2.4, 1973

A legend is born

BY THE EARLY 1960s THE 356 WAS beginning to show its age, and Ferry Porsche was keen to develop a successor. He got his son, Ferdinand Alexander Porsche – commonly known as 'Butzi' – to style the new sports car. The brief was simple – the car had to be better than the 356 in every way, and be more of a GT tourer than its somewhat basic predecessor. The design Butzi came up with was labelled Type 7 and this was to form the basis of what was to become the 911.

A new engine was developed which, while retaining the air-cooled flat-six design, now had six cylinders and was made from aluminium to reduce weight (it still hung over the rear of the car and so keeping the weight down helped handling). This was a technologically advanced unit with a dry sump, overhead camshafts, 1991cc capacity and six Solex carburettors. With an output of 130bhp the new engine put the 911 in a different category to the four-cylinder 356. Going through a new five-speed gearbox, the power meant the 911 could reach 60mph in just 8.5 seconds and reach a top speed of 131mph – impressive figures, indeed, for the early 1960s.

The new body was larger and sleeker than that of the 356, with room in the back for two children. Below it, the space-saving torsion-bar suspension remained, but at the front was a new MacPherson strut layout which, nonetheless, left room for a good-sized luggage compartment. The rear suspension consisted of semi-trailing arms, while brakes were discs all round.

The exciting new Porsche was unveiled at the 1963 Frankfurt motor show, to great excitement. No one doubted that the car was technologically advanced but there were some who complained that it had lost the raw appeal of the 356 – a complaint that some enthusiasts would (and still do) make each time a new Porsche came out over the years. Porsche labelled its creation '901' but Peugeot claimed it had the rights to all tags with a central zero, so it was hastily renamed '911'. And so a motoring legend was born.

The 911 gradually evolved over the years, getting more and more powerful and better equipped to cope with changing world demands. However, it remained very much based on that

BELOW 911 Carrera 3.0, 1977

first 2.0-litre car right up until 1996, when an all-new water-cooled version came along.

Right from the start the 911 was a success, and found plenty of buyers. It

ABOVE 911SC, 1977

wasn't perfect, though, and early examples soon gained a reputation for somewhat wayward handling – lift off the throttle partway through a bend and the

car could all too easily spin. This was a characteristic of the rear-engine layout and Porsche put a lot of effort into compensating for it and, before long, the 911 handling was faultless in all but extreme conditions. However, the damage was done and even today people think that 911s don't handle 'properly' because the engine is in the 'wrong place'.

The 911 was very obviously a more expensive and more powerful car than the 356, so it was planned right from the start to offer a budget version, that would appeal to those people who would previously have bought a 356.

That car appeared in 1965 and was called the 912. It shared the same body as the 911 but was powered by a simpler four-cylinder engine – the 1582cc unit which was used in the last of the 356s and developed a modest 90bhp. The 912 sold mainly to the US market until it was discontinued in 1969 (although the concept returned briefly in 1975 as the 912E). The 912 was popular with buyers who wanted to look as if they were driving a 911 but without the expense.

A deal with Volkswagen

ONCE THE 911 WAS AN ESTABLISHED success, Porsche was keen to expand its range and the obvious choice was an entry-level car that would replace the 912. In the mid-1960s, Ferry Porsche began discussions with Volkswagen to plan a car that would open both marques up to new markets – the latter had only the Beetle at this time.

The result of this collaboration appeared in 1969 and was known as the Porsche 914, although outside North America it also sported a VW badge. The 914 had distinctive angular lines and a removable Targa roof. Its midmounted engine was a new Volkswagen design with four horizontally opposed cylinders and air cooling. With a modest capacity of 1679cc it produced 80bhp, which endowed the car with a top speed of 110mph and a 0-60mph time of 12.4 seconds.

The 914 was designed by an outside company, Gugelot Design and built by coachbuilder Karmann. Combined with the Volkswagen engine, this immedi-

ately led to criticisms that the 914 wasn't a 'true' Porsche and, besides, the performance was nothing to write home about. Porsche addressed the latter by offering the 914/6 which featured a 110bhp flat-six 911 engine. This car dashed to 60mph in 8.8 seconds and went onto a top speed of 122mph.

Sadly, though, despite almost 120,000 sales, the 914 never really found its niche, despite being relatively popular in North America. In 1976, due in part to the introduction of the Volkswagen Golf, the 914 was discontinued.

ABOVE 914/6, 1969

A move to the front

IN 1972 FERRY PORSCHE, WHILE retaining overall ownership, passed over the running of his company to Dr Ernst Fuhrmann, a man who was keen to explore new markets for Porsche. In particular, Fuhrmann was adamant that an entry-level car was required, to replace the 914 while, in time, something had to be done to replace the aging 911.

For the entry-level car, Porsche again turned to Volkswagen. This time Porsche looked after the design and development, while Volkswagen supplied many of the mechanical parts. Porsche wanted the car to carry its badge, of course, but for a while its partner was insisting that the new sports car be sold as a Volkswagen. Thankfully, the oil crisis of 1974 tempered Volkswagen's enthusiasm and Porsche ended up buying up the entire project, albeit then sub-contracting back to Volkswagen to build the car at the old NSU factory at Neckarsulm.

The result was the Porsche 924 which went on sale in 1976. This was a complete departure from previous Porsches, in that it featured a front-mounted, water-cooled engine. This 1984cc was essentially an Audi unit which Porsche tweaked to give an output of 125bhp. The power went to a rear mounted gear-

BELOW 924, 1976

box/transaxle which was initially four-speed, but a five-speed version soon followed. The advantage of this layout was that it gave the car a near-perfect weight balance that helped the handling.

The 924 was clothed in a pretty two-plus-two bodyshell that had room for children in the back. What's more, it featured a large glass hatchback that gave excellent access to the relatively large rear boot. This really was a practical sports car.

The 924 remained in production until 1985 and was a massive success for Porsche, with over 110,000 examples being built. Its basic form would continue into the 1990s as the 944 and then the 968. The 924 was also offered in Turbo form between 1979 and 1983.

Goodbye 911?

ERNST FUHRMANN WAS SURE that the 911's days were numbered; after all it had been around since 1964 and, in the 1970s, was essentially the same body shape as it had always been. He maintained that a replacement was required, and it would have to be a larger, more powerful and more luxurious car – a true grand tourer. It must also boast the latest technology.

In 1977, then, Porsche unveiled the car that it hoped would replace the 911. And what a car it was! The 928, as it was known, looked like nothing else. At a time when most cars were boxy and sharp-edged, the 928 with its curvaceous body, which was styled by Tony Lapine, looked like something from out of space.

In many ways, it followed the form of the 924, in that it was front-engined with a rear-mounted automatic gearbox (a manual option followed), had two-plus-two accommodation and a lifting hatchback.

However, where the 924 was somewhat underpowered, the 928 had more than enough. The engine was a Porsche-designed all-aluminium, 4474cc V8 with water cooling and Bosch fuel injection. It produced a healthy 240bhp – enough to rocket the big car from 0-60mph in 8.1 seconds and on to a top speed of 142mph.

The 928 had a spacious (for front passengers, at least), well-trimmed cockpit with all the electronic trickery expected of a luxury car. It was undoubtedly a capable machine yet very much a grand tourer, not a pure sports car, and that meant the 928 never really

caught on with many Porsche enthusiasts. It was also a very expensive car, both to buy and to run.

The 928 remained in production until 1995, during which time it found many friends and was treated to a number of updates, included engine improvements that upped power to 330bhp. However the car never achieved what it was meant to do – replace the 911, which continued to outsell it.

BELOW 928, 1988

Turbo power

WHEN THE 928 WAS LAUNCHED, IT was a million miles from the 911, in looks, comfort and technology. Although the 911 had evolved over the years it was, essentially, still the same car it was when it appeared in 1963. And yet people continued to choose it in preference to the newer 928.

One of the reasons for the 911's success was its appearance – that body shape was unmistakeable. And it became even more distinctive in 1975 when the first 911 Turbo was introduced. With extended front and rear wheel arches and a massive whaletail spoiler, this was a 911 like no other. The original pretty lines had given way to pure aggression – the 911 Turbo simply oozed power.

BELOW 911 Turbo, 1975

There was more to the Turbo than wild looks, though. Under that rear spoiler, the 3.0-litre engine was fitted with a single KKK turbocharger that upped power to an incredible (for the day) 260bhp.

That meant the car could hit 60mph in just six seconds and go onto a top speed of 155mph. Sadly, though, Porsche didn't think to uprate the brakes to suit until 1978 when a revised 911 Turbo came out.

This new version not only had suitable stopping capabilities, it also boasted a 3.3-litre engine that could produce 300bhp. From there on, there was no stopping the 911 Turbo which has continued to be Porsche's flagship to this day, and favourite for schoolboys' bedroom walls.

The legend lives on

BY THE EARLY 1980s PORSCHE realised that the 911 wasn't going to go away, and so it began to make plans to bring it up to date. Ernst Fuhrmann, who'd strived to replace the model, retired at the end of 1981, still claiming that the 911 had had its day. In his place came Peter Schutz, who could see that customers wanted 911s, so that's what he gave them.

An all-new 911 was going to take time, though, so as an interim to fuel demand, Porsche introduced the Carrera 3.2. Oddly, this car was not badged a 911 – a tradition that continues to this day. It was, though, very clearly a 911 in that it used the same bodyshell as previous versions, albeit fitted with the impact-absorbing bumpers which first appeared in the 1970s so that the car would conform to US safety regulations.

The engine, too, was carried over, but enlarged to 3164cc and fitted with, for the first time, a Bosch Motronic engine management system. This, combined with other changes, produced a power output of 231bhp, yet the engine was more economical than that of previous 911s.

The Carrera 3.2 was a great sale success during the economic boom of the mid-1980s; in 1985 alone some 21,000 were built. The model continued until 1989.

BELOW 911 Carrera 3.2, 1986

Supercar

IT WAS ARGUED BY SOME THAT the reason Porsche didn't develop the 911 much in the early 1980s was because it was devoting its attention to a very special car – the 959. Still technologically advanced today, the 959 was clearly based on a 911 but was something quite extraordinary.

The 959 was originally conceived as a homologation special to enable Porsche to compete in Group B motorsport, which meant everything from the Le Mans 24-hour race to the Paris Dakar rally. The rules demanded that Porsche build 200 road-going cars so the company took the opportunity to create a showcase for its design and engineering skills.

At the heart of the 959, which first went on show in prototype form in 1983, was a very advanced flat-six engine with a capacity of 2850cc. Unlike traditional 911 engines, this one had water-cooled cylinder heads, which were required to cope with the heat generated by the power created by twin turbochargers. The engine – which had a relatively small capacity – produced an astonishing 450bhp.

The power was fed to all four wheels using a transmission system that Porsche developed itself. This was a complex mechanism that allowed the torque normally to be split 40/60 in favour of the rear wheels, yet increasing to 20/80 under acceleration. There was also a control in the cabin that let you select one of four programmes to suit

the road conditions – dry, wet, snow and lock. The last option locked the differential.

Another cabin control allowed you to select the ride height. Yes, the 959 had a

sophisticated suspension system that used coil springs instead of the 911's torsion bars, not to mention two dampers per wheel and hydraulic height adjustment. Also new was an ABS braking system and even tyre pressure sensors which alerted the driver if one of the tyres was running soft.

The 959's bodyshell used carbonfibre and Kevlar to reduce weight, and was developed in a wind tunnel to create a stunning shape which still looks modern today. The only thing that perhaps let the car down was the interior, which was pretty much standard 911, albeit leather-clad.

However, the interior's shortcomings became irrelevant when the car's performance was used to the full. With a top speed of 197mph and a 0-60mph time of just 3.9-seconds, the 959 was unbeatable, and remains one of the world's fastest cars today. However, despite the phenomenal performance it remained a comfortable, safe and civilised car to drive.

Aggressive facelift

WHILE PORSCHE WAS WOOING the super-rich with its 959, at the other end of the market things just got very much better for buyers. In 1982 the 924 was substantially updated and named 944. New boss Peter Schutz was keen to get fresh business and, once and for all, put paid to comments that the 924 wasn't a real Porsche.

The company had been working on a new engine for the 924 since the late 1970s and Schutz could see the potential in a more powerful, front-engined car to woo customers who weren't interested in the traditional 911, but instead wanted a modern, relatively affordable sports car with the all-important Porsche badge. Image was everything in this market, so the new car was given bulging front and rear wheel arches (based on those of the Carrera GT racecar) to make it appear much more aggressive than the somewhat petite 924.

The engine itself was revolutionary. In an ideal world, Porsche would have fit-

ABOVE 944, 1985

ted a straight-six or V6 engine, but the former wouldn't fit under the bonnet, while to keep costs down Porsche wanted to use a single 928 cylinder head, which dictated a straight-four. The new, all-alloy engine had a capacity of 2479cc – large for an inherently unbalanced four-cylinder unit. To ensure that the engine ran as smoothly as a six, Porsche fitted two counter-rotating balance-shafts inside the block; an idea thought up at the start of the 20th century by British car builder Lanchester.

The engine, with its 163bhp output, transformed the Porsche, giving respectable performance figures of 0-60mph in 8.4 seconds, coupled with a top speed of 131mph. No one could say this wasn't a true Porsche! Buyers agreed, and the 944 was a tremendous sales success for Porsche, especially in the USA. To put it into context, in 1981 the company sold a total of 28,000 cars worldwide – of all its models. However, in 1983 it shifted over 26,500 944s alone! The 944 was updated and developed until it was discontinued in 1989. In 1985 a Turbo version was introduced, with a 220bhp (increasing to 250bhp in 1988) turbocharged version of the four-cylinder engine and even more aggressive looks.

BELOW 944, 1986

New life

BY THE END OF THE 1980s, the world was in recession and the 911, like many high-performance cars, was out of favour with buyers – in 1989 just 7000 Carrera 3.2s were sold. This was partly down to the economy, but there was no getting away from the fact that the 911 was dated and its image had been somewhat tainted by the 'yuppie' generation. Porsche was in trouble and new boss, Heinz Branitzski, who replaced Peter Schutz in 1987, was struggling to keep the company afloat.

It was obvious that an all-new 911 was required, but there wasn't the money – or the time – to do this, so Porsche's engineers were charged with doing the best with what they had. Luckily, they had the experience of the 959 supercar to draw on and they made good use of this in giving the 911 its first major make-over.

The new car was called Carrera 4 and given the internal model number 964,

ABOVE 911 Carrera 4, 1990

and it's still referred to as such by enthusiasts. Porsche claimed it was 87 percent new. The big news was that, as the name suggests, the Carrera 4 had four-wheel-drive. This was a much simpler system than that used on the 959, but Porsche drew upon that technology to develop a transmission for the 964. The gearbox was an evolution of that used in the last Carrera 3.2s.

Feeding the transmission was a 3600cc engine which, again, was loosely based on the previous unit, but updated and improved to give an output of 250bhp.

The suspension was all new. Out went the quirky torsion bars, which dated back to the Volkswagen Beetle of the 1930s, and in came conventional coil springs and dampers. Also, for the first time on a production 911, the brakes were helped by ABS.

The body shape was basically the same as that of previous 911s, but looked more modern with its integral plastic bumpers and an innovative rear spoiler that sat flush with the body at rest, to retain the car's pure lines, but raised up at speed to give extra down-force when required. Inside, the traditional 911 dash remained, but was updated with new finishes and an array of warning lights.

A rear-wheel-drive Carrera 2 followed in 1990, as did a Turbo version. The new 964-model ran to 1993 and gave the 911 a boost, but it was not enough to drag Porsche out of its financial difficulties.

Nice try

PORSCHE WAS IN FINANCIAL turmoil in the early 1990s, and sales of all its models were struggling. Even the popular entry-level 944 was failing to find buyers, so Porsche took the decision to give the car a major overall and rename it 968.

The 968 was very clearly evolved from the 944, but was treated to a fresh new nose with exposed flip-up headlamps that made it look much more modern. The rear end was also cleaned up with an integral plastic bumper and new light clusters.

Yet the 968, which arrived in 1991, was more than just a face-lifted 944. Under the bonnet the 3.0-litre engine was considerably reworked to produce 240bhp, and was linked to a new six-speed gearbox. The suspension was revised, too, and the 968 was widely hailed as one of the best-handling Porsches to date, especially in its stripped-out ClubSport form. Sadly, it was not enough and the 968 was not a sales success, and less than 13,000 had been built by the time the model was discontinued in 1995.

BELOW 968 Cabriolet, 1991

Last of the line

WHILE STRUGGLING TO REMAIN afloat in the early 1990s, Porsche knew

In 1992, Porsche had yet another new boss, the 39-year-old Wenderlin Wiedeking, who had previously been Production Director. One of his tasks was to reduce costs, and he was ruthless in reducing the workforce – both on the shop floor and in management – but he also wanted to make the cars less costly to build. To this end, he brought in Japanese advisors to change the production methods for the next generation of 911. This new car was code-named 993 and each one took an incredible 40 hours less time to build than the previous 911. It also required less factory space and less inventory.

However, it was no good whatsoever having a car that was less costly to build if no one wanted to buy it, so the 993 was given a fresh new look. Penned by British designer, Tony Hatter, the 993 brought the 911's lines bang up to date, with swept-back headlamps in lower front wings, and more curvaceous, sensual lines. There was no doubting that the

ABOVE Assembly line – building the next Porsche

that the 911 was key to its success. The 964 version had certainly helped gener-ate fresh interest in the model, but by modern standards it was expensive to build and barely profitable.

new car looked stunning, yet at the same time unmistakeably a 911.

Mechanically, the 993 was based broadly on the previous 964, but with an updated engine and a six-speed gearbox. In a departure from other 911s, the rear suspension was an all-new multi-link set-up that improved both ride and handling.

The 993-model 911 was produced from 1994 to 1997 and was offered in four- and two-wheel-drive derivatives, while a Turbo version came along in 1993, with even more curvaceous lines. The 993 was a success – it was a great car to look at and to drive and – more importantly – it brought back customers to Porsche and generated much needed cash to carry the company forward into the 21st century. What's more, it has gone down in history as the last – and many say best – of the air-cooled 911s. That said, someone who wasn't totally happy with the new look was the now elderly Ferry Porsche, who complained that you could no longer see the front wings from the driver's seat – something he'd always maintained was an essential characteristic of a 911.

The next generation

WITH THE 993-MODEL CAR Porsche had pushed the traditional 911 concept to the limit. It would be hard to squeeze any more power from the air-cooled engine, and even harder to make it comply with new noise and emissions regulations dictated by European and North American governments from the 1990s. What's more, the design was undoubtedly starting to show its age. Porsche aficionados might put up with the illogical dashboard layout, offset pedals and cramped rear seats, but other buyers were less forgiving and were being tempted away by more modern offerings from other manufacturers.

So in 1991 the decision was made to develop an all-new 911 for the 21st century. The plan was to come up with a joint platform for both the 996 (which was the factory's designation for the 911 project) and a new entry-level car code-named 986 (which was to become the Boxster), using as many shared parts as possible. Money was tight and a large-volume car would help carry the devel-

opment of the more expensive 911.

The 996 had to be rear-engined to be a true 911, of course, while it was decided to make the Boxster mid-engined, so the two cars were basically identical from the front bulkhead forwards, but in other respects quite distinct. The new 911 was larger then its predecessor (some 19cm longer) to improve accommodation and to make room for the water-cooling radiators. It also had much smoother, less fussy lines to improve aerodynamics and give a more modern appearance, while at the same time retaining the trademark 911 signatures.

Porsche knew that its air-cooled engine had reached its sell-by date, but wanted to retain the 911 character with a flat-six engine rather than, say, a V8. The solution, then, was an all-new water-cooled, four valves per cylinder design with a displacement of 3.4-litres and an output

of 300bhp. Water-cooling meant that the engine could be made to run quieter, cope with more power, and be more efficient. Again to save money, many engine components were shared with the smaller 2.5-litre Boxster unit, which produced 204bhp. For both cars, the power went through a new six-speed gearbox or an optional five-speed Tiptronic automatic transmission.

ABOVE Boxster 2.5L, 1997

A BRIEF HISTORY OF PORSCHE

Inside, the new 911 and Boxster were also related. In the case of the new 996, out went the old classic 911 layout to be replaced by a modern array of overlapping dials and an easy-to-reach centre console. The driving position was much improved and the rear seats had more space. The 911 had never before been so refined and comfortable.

The mid-engine Boxster, meanwhile, was strictly a two-seater and had an electrically operated folding roof that disappeared neatly behind the seats to give true open-air motoring. The dash design was similar to that of the 911.

The Boxster was unveiled in 1996 and was an instant success. There were no doubts this time around that this entry-level car was a real Porsche, both in looks and performance, even though its appearance wasn't as radical as that of the original show car.

RIGHT Boxster S, 1999

In 1999 it was updated with a more powerful 2.7-litre engine and the Boxster S was introduced with a 3.2-litre powerplant. Further updates followed in later years, as the Boxster continued to break all sales record to help establish Porsche as the world's most profitable car manufacturer.

The new 996-model 911 was introduced in 1997, with the first cars sold the following year, and was also a great success. Critics said it wasn't a 'true' 911 because it didn't have an air-cooled engine or a traditional appearance, inside or out Indeed, some said the lines were somewhat bland. However, the fact of the matter was that the 996 was the car that the market demanded. By making the 911 less quirky and more comfortable and easy to drive, Porsche opened the car up to a much wider market and the 996 became the best-selling Porsche to date.

Like its predecessors, the 996 was offered in Carrera 4 and Carrera (rear-wheel-drive) formats, as well as a stunning Turbo, which was hailed by many as the 'best car in the world' with its 420bhp engine driving all four wheels. The 996-model 911 range received various updates and additions until it was discontinued in 2004.

Super GT

WHEN PORSCHE BUILT THE 959 supercar in the 1980s it served as a showcase to demonstrate what the company's designers could come up. For 2000, Porsche returned to the supercar concept, but this time took a very different approach.

The new car was the stunning Carrera GT, which first appeared at the Paris motor show in 2000 as a concept. Such

RIGHT AND
BELOW RIGHT
Carrera GT, 2005

BELOW Carrera GT
interior, 2005

was the response to the show car, that Porsche decided to put it into limited production, from 2003.

Unlike the 959, the Carrera GT shunned high technology four-wheel-drive and active suspension, in favour of pure power and light weight. At the heart of the car was a mid-mounted V10 engine with a capacity of 5733cc that developed an incredible 612bhp – and it wasn't even turbocharged! The power drove the rear wheels only via a six-speed gearbox and unique ceramic clutch. Brakes, too, were massive ceramic discs with six-piston calipers acting on them.

However, despite the phenomenal power of the engine, Porsche went to great lengths to make the Carrera GT as light as possible, to maximise performance. To this end, the car had a carbonfibre monocoque bodyshell, which was beautifully finished with bare, polished carbonfibre on show around the massive engine compartment. The car was strictly a two-seater, with a comfortable, but not overly luxurious, interior.

Removable, Targa-style roof panels –
made with carbonfibre – could be stored
in the front luggage compartment to give
open-top motoring.

The result of this weight saving meant
that the Carrera GT came in at just
1380kg. And that, combined with the
power, meant that it would accelerate
from standstill to 62mph in just 3.9 seconds. Top speed was 205mph!

Going off-road

DESPITE THE SUCCESS OF THE Boxster and 996-model 911, at the start of the 21st century Porsche's boss, Wendelin Wiedeking was eager to expand into new, lucrative markets so that his company was not having to rely solely on the increasingly competitive

sports car market. Porsche was a powerful brand name and Wiedeking wanted to exploit to the fullest.

The new direction the company chose was controversial; it wanted to exploit the growing enthusiasm for luxury four-wheel-drive sport utility vehicles (SUV), a market that was traditionally led by the Range Rover.

Amazingly, this idea was not new, because in the early 1970s Ferry Porsche had considered a four-by-four, four-seater car, based loosely on the 911, that could be driven on or off road. Even back then he could see the benefits of diversifying into other markets, but his management team did not agree and the project was shelved. Sadly, Ferry Porsche died in 1988 but he would surely have been pleased to see his concept being resurrected for the new century.

Porsche did, for a while, have a few discussions with Mercedes Benz to develop a

Porsche version of the G-Wagen, but in the end it was decided to partner with Volkswagen for the project, which was coded E1 (Porsche had just about run out of '900' numbers) and MAC (Multi Activity Vehicle) in the case of the Volkswagen version

Porsche did most of the research and development of the new cars, for which it was paid by Volkswagen, and the result was the Porsche Cayenne and Volkswagen Toureg, which shared many common parts.

The Cayenne was designed to excel both on and off road, and as such was available with optional air suspension. This allowed the ride height to be varied as required, from a very low 'Load' setting for getting in and out of the stationary vehicle, 'Normal' for everyday driving, 'Low' for high-speed motorway cruising, and 'High' for tackling rough off-road terrain. In addition, the driver could adjust the damper settings to give a soft, normal or sporty ride.

The key to any off-roader is its transmission system and here the Cayenne didn't disappoint. Available with manual or automatic gearchange, the system could vary the amount of torque supplied to the front and rear wheels as

LEFT Cayenne SUV, 2005

A BRIEF HISTORY OF PORSCHE

ABOVE Cayenne rolling off the production line

form this produced 340bhp, while the engine in the top of the range Turbo model pumped out a hefty 450bhp, allowing the car to reach 60mph in 5.6 seconds and carry on to a top speed of 165mph. Not bad for a big off-roader weighing 2355kg!

The Cayenne, which was launched in 2002, was undoubtedly a well-engineered machine, but its looks were rather less well received. It was designed to have the Porsche 'family look' which is particularly apparent around the front end and the rear quarter windows, which have hints of 911 about them. Unfortunately, the shape was not a success, with it being christened the 'Porker' by unkind members of the press. Nonetheless the car –

required, and a low-ratio setting gave the driver extra control when off-roading.

Power came from an all-new 4511cc V8 engine with twin overhead camshafts and four valves per cylinder. In standard

which was built at a new factory at Leipzig, in eastern Germany – proved popular with buyers who wanted the prestige of the Porsche badge on a big and fashionable off-roader.

Back to the future

AS GOOD AS THE 996-MODEL 911 was, right from its introduction it was criticised, mainly by die-hard Porsche enthusiasts. It was, they said, bland-looking and lacked the essential 911 character. Porsche's designers obviously took the comments seriously when they were planning a successor to the best-selling 996 range.

That new car was the 997-model 911 Carrera, launched in 2004, which very obviously drew on the shape of the previous 993-model car for inspiration.. The wings became more shapely and the car less slab-sided, while at the front the large, oval-shaped projector head-lamps had an unashamed 993 influence. The indicators were housed in the front bumper; again, as per 993.

BELOW 911 Carrera S, 2005

ABOVE 911 Carrera S
dashboard, 2005

some of that traditional 911 sound-track. The more powerful Carrera S version had a 3.8-litre engine that developed 355bhp. In both case, the power went to the rear wheels via a six-speed gearbox, while an automatic Tiptronic S was optional. Four-wheel-drive was not offered at the car's launch.

An exciting new option was PASM (Porsche Active Suspension Management). This gave the driver a choice of two suspension settings, simply by pressing a button on the centre console. Normal mode was for standard on-road driving and offered a comfortable ride quality; but when the system detected that the car was being driven and cornered hard, the damper settings automatically firmed up to compensate. By contrast, the Sports mode gave a harder ride for optimum handling on twisty roads or the racetrack. PASM effectively gave you two cars in one – a comfortable everyday tourer and a honed track machine.

Another innovation was Sports Chrono Package Plus. This gave another button on the centre console which, when activated, changed the engine management 'maps' to offer more immediate throttle response and a higher rev limit.

While the exterior changes were an evolution of the 996's lines, the interior was all-new, albeit with a nod to the 993 (and earlier) dash layouts. The dash was more angular than that of the 996, and featured a large screen in the console for PCM (Porsche Communication Management).

The standard 997 Carrera had essentially the same 3.6-litre engine as the 996, but it was fine-tuned to give an increased power output of 325bhp (a modest 5bhp increase), while a new exhaust system brought back at least

The new 997-model 911 Carrera gave the perfect combination of 911 traditions with 21st century technology and was well-received by press and buyers alike. While being very obviously a 911, in many ways it was a million miles from the 2.0-litre car that started the model off in 1963. That said, back then the 911 was as technologically advanced for its day as the 997 was in 2004.

BELOW 911 Carrera S from the rear, 2005

Back to basics

FOR SOME ENTHUSIASTS, THE 911 lost some of its appeal as it grew larger, heavier and more complex. It was, they said, no longer a true sports car, but more a long-distance tourer. Porsche took these comments to heart and, while the 911 was the right car for the market, they could see there was a demand for a smaller, purer sports car.

Called the Cayman S, this coupe was based on the Boxster but powered by a

BELOW Cayman S, 2005

mid-mounted 3.4-litre flat-six engine (essentially the same as that in the 911) that produced 295bhp. Looking not unlike a mini 911, with curvaceous and muscular lines, the two-seater was designed to be as light as possible and to offer pure driving pleasure.

The future

PORSCHE HAS COME A LONG WAY since Ferry Porsche and his father designed the first 356 back in 1948. Yet put one of those early cars next to a modern 911, Boxster or Cayman and it's very obvious that the new cars share the same DNA as that first Porsche. And that is one of the appeals of Porsche; it's stayed true to its founder's principles, which is to produce innovative, exciting, beautiful and practical sports cars.

Porsche as a company started the 21st century in extraordinarily good financial shape. Its cars were selling well throughout the world and it had the money to invest in new product lines, while at the same time consolidating what it already has.

LEFT Checking the paint on a Boxster in the workshop

The company knows now that the 911 is central to its product line. The 997-version will be replaced towards the end of the century's first decade, probably by an all-new model. It has been hinted that the traditional flat-six engine will be replaced by the V8 that's used in the Cayenne. Only time will tell, but what is certain is that the car will be unmistakably a 911, as will every 911 that follows it.

There is also a possibility that the company will produce a four-seater saloon car that encapsulates Porsche's core values of sportiness and technological excellence.

In 2002, the company's CEO, Dr Wendelin Wiedeking – who's contract runs to 2007 – stated that he wanted to see Porsche producing 100,000 cars a year. However, he insisted that Porsche would remain an exclusive brand building niche models.

One thing is certain, though, whatever Porsche decides to build in the future we can be sure that they will some of the best cars on the planet – to look at and to drive.

Porsche milestones

1875: Ferdinand Porsche born

1900: Lohner-Porsche electric car shown at the Paris Expo

1932: Ferdinand Porsche sets up his design company

1936: Type 36 Volkswagen prototypes built

1938: Volkswagen factory built at Wolfsburg

1947: Ferry Porsche designs Type 360 Cisitalia Grand Prix car

1948: First Porsche 356 built in Gmünd, Austria

1950: Porsche moves to Stuttgart to productionise the 356

1951: Ferdinand Porsche Senior dies, aged 75

1951: A Porsche 356 wins the 1100cc category at the Le Mans 24-hour race

1956: The 10,000th Porsche 356 is built

1961: Work starts on a new six-cylinder Porsche, with a body designed by Ferdinand 'Butzi' Porsche

1963: The Porsche 911 is unveiled at the Frankfurt motor show

BELOW Porsche alloy wheel, featuring that all important logo

A BRIEF HISTORY OF PORSCHE

1964: Production of the Porsche 911 begins

1965: Four-cylinder 912 introduced

1969: Porsche unveils its entry-level 914 and 914/6 models

1970: Porsche 917 racecar appears with 4.5-litre V12 engine and becomes an outstanding success

1972: Porsche becomes a public company, with Ferry Porsche as Chairman of the Supervisory Board

1972: Porsche unveils the 911Carrera 2.7 RS, which was to become one of the most sought-after cars of all time

1975: 911 Turbo goes on sale

1976: Entry-level 924 becomes available, with a front-mounted water-cooled four-cylinder engine

1977: Porsche introduces the V8-powered 928 grand-tourer

1982: The Porsche 956 racecar begins its career to become the most successful racing car of all time

1982: Porsche 944 introduced, based on 924 but with more power and wider arches

1985: Porsche launches the high-tech 959 supercar

1986: A modified 959 becomes the first sports car to win the Paris-Dakar rally

1989: Four-wheel-drive 964-model 911 Carrera 4 introduced

1990: The 911 is offered for the first time with Tiptronic transmission, giving a choice of manual or automatic changes

RIGHT 944 Turbo front wing, 1988

A BRIEF HISTORY OF PORSCHE

1991: Porsche 968 introduced, based on 944

1993: Boxster concept car shown at the Detroit motor show

1993: 993-model 911 Carrera introduced, with new multilink rear suspension

1996: Mid-engined Boxster goes into production

1997: Porsche unveils the all-new 996-model 911 with water-cooled engine

2000: Carrera GT concept supercar shown at the Paris motor show

2002: Porsche launches Cayenne SUV with V8 engine and four-wheel-drive

2004: New 997-model 911 returns to more traditional 911 appearance

2005: Cayman S launched, based on Boxster underpinnings

ABOVE 911 GT3 rear end detail, 2003

Chapter 2

Porsche in Motorsport

BELOW Ferdinand
Porsche Snr pictured
in 1940

BELOW Ferdinand
Porsche Snr pictured
in 1940

Racing start

RACING HAS ALWAY'S BEEN IN Porsche's bloodline right back to the early 1900s, when Ferdinand Porsche entered a lightweight version of his revolutionary electric-powered Lohner-Porsche in a hillclimb event at the Semmering Pass in the Austrian Alps on 23rd September 1900. He broke the previous record for electric cars by fifty percent, with an average speed of 25mph. Over the next few years, Porsche developed his car and entered it successfully in other similar events.

356 breaks out

FERDINAND PORSCHE BECAME involved in many other racecar projects for other companies up until the time he and his son Ferry started producing their own cars – the Porsche 356 – in 1948. And it wasn't long before that was pressed into service on the track. The very first prototype, 356-001, was raced by Herbert Kaes in a local event at Innsbruck, Austria, in July 1948. The car won its class and went down in history as the first victory for a Porsche.

Once the 356 went into production-proper in 1950, owners started to race their cars in local rallies and other events. Porsche gave whatever support it could to these privateers, and soon realised the marketing potential in motorsport, arguing that it was more effective and less expensive than advertising. So, in 1950 a decision was made to compete in the Le Mans 24-hour endurance event.

The three cars that were prepared were, in fact, aluminium-bodied examples built at Gmünd before the move to Stuttgart. These were lighter than the production steel cars and of less com-

mercial value to the company. Modified engines produced 46mph, enough to propel the cars to just over 100mph. Sadly, two of the cars were destroyed in accidents before race, so only one 356 was able to compete. This car, driven by Auguste Veulliet and Edmond

BELOW 356 at Le Mans, 1953

Mouche, won the 1100cc class and finished 20th overall, with an average speed of 73mph.

The Gmünd coupes raced again at Le Mans in 1951 and 1952, again with some success. Also in 1952 two 356s competed in the Carrera Panamericana in Mexico. This 2000-mile race ran north along the new Pan American highway and was in its third year. One car, driven by Paul von Metternich, finished eighth overall, despite suffering from a number of mechanical problems. The second car was piloted by Count Konstantin von Berckheim and retired with transmission failure. This race was the start of a long association the Carrera Panamericana and the establishment of a now-famous Porsche model name.

BELOW 356 in The Monte Carlo Rally, 1954

Pure-bred 550

IN 1953, PORSCHE'S VERY FIRST purpose-made racecar appeared. The Type 550 had more in common with the first 356/001 than in the production version. It was mid-engined, for starters and used a lightweight ladder-frame chassis clothed in a sleek aluminium bodyshell. The engine was a 1500cc flat-four that, on the first examples, produced 98bhp. On its maiden run the first 550 (dubbed 550-01) was driven to class victory by Helm Glöckler at the Nurbürgring in May 1953. The following month, a 550 won the 1500cc class at Le Mans and set a new record.

The 550 was developed and went on to win numerous races, including taking the top four places at the Nurbürgring in 1954. In 1956 the updated 550A RS, which was lighter and more powerful, won the famous Targa Florio race, driven by Huschke von Hanstein and Umberto Maglioli, despite being a hastily prepared campaign. This was the first of a number of victories for Porsche at this event, which inspired the name of the company's now famous removable roof system.

By 1957 Porsche's racing car had evolved into the 718 RSK, which had a revised front suspension to improve handling and allow a lower, more aerodynamic front end. A choice of 1600cc and 1700cc flat-four engines were available. In 1958 718s came third at Sebring, second overall in the Targa Florio, and third and fourth overall at

BELOW 550 Spyder, 1955

wheelbase was longer to improve handling, while power from the 1578cc flat-four was up to 160bhp – not bad for a car weighing just 550kg. First time out was at Sebring, where RS60s took first and second place. And then Graham Hill drove one to victory in that year's Targa Florio.

Formula One foray

IN 1961, PORSCHE HAD ENTERED Formula One Grand Prix racing with the 718-based RS61 cars. Drivers were Jo Bonnier, Hans Herrman and Dan Gurney. Unfortunately, the team could do no better than three second places through the season and the following year the cars were replaced with the Type 804, which was specially built for Formula One. The car was powered by a new engine that followed Porsche tradition by being air-cooled and having a flat-eight configuration. It had a capacity of 1494cc (to comply with Formula One regulations) but was designed with future capacities of up to 2000cc in

Le Mans. Not a bad start for the car! The following year was even better, with a win at the Targa Florio, while five 718s made the top ten at Sebring.

New regulations for 1960 demanded that racers had a closer resemblance to road-going cars, with a higher windscreen and luggage space. Porsche responded with the 718 RS60. The

Yet the company realised that it had to come up with something new to remain competitive.

The solution was the all-new 904, a beautiful-looking car designed by Butzi Porsche, who also penned the 911. It featured a glassfibre body over a ladder-frame chassis and was designed to be fitted with either a four-, six-

LEFT Jo Bonnier receiving instructions

BELOW 904, 1965

mind. The cars were reasonably successful, winning one race in the season and came fifth in the Manufacturers' Challenge. However, new regulations and a change of direction at Porsche meant that this was the only year it competed in Formula One because the company withdrew to concentrate on sports-car racing instead.

Beautiful 904

BY 1962, THE 356-BASED RACE-cars were reaching the end of their competitive lives. The final incarnation was the two-litre, eight-cylinder 718GTR which gave Porsche yet another victory at the Targa Florio.

or eight-cylinder flat-six engine. Fitted with the 200bhp four-cylinder unit, 904s took first and second places at the Targa Florio in 1964, and managed the same at Le Mans, with all five entered cars finishing the event. The 904 – and its immediate successors – was undoubtedly successful, and ran in a number of different forms, but the world of motorsport was moving away from modified road cars to purpose-built racers. Porsche had no choice but to move on, with its sights set on big things.

The ultimate – 917

PORSCHE HAD BEEN COMPETING at Le Mans for many years and had had much success within its class, but had never managed an overall win. However, by 1969 it had a brand-new car with which to compete. That was the now legendary 917, said by some to be the greatest Porsche of all time. When the 917 was unveiled at the 1969 Geneva Salon, it came as a complete surprise – no one was expecting Porsche to come up with something as radical as this.

The 917 was a huge car, developed by Ferdinand Piëch, consisting of a lightweight aluminium spaceframe chassis topped by an aerodynamically efficient glassfibre bodyshell. The car's shape was developed in a wind-tunnel, which led to the distinctive long tail, which gave a drag co-efficient of just 0.33 (a short-tail version came in at 0.40). Fins on each front wing tilted as the suspension moved to help keep the car on the ground. To save weight, much of the suspension – including the coil springs – were made of titanium.

However, the really exciting thing about the 917 was its engine, which had the internal type number 912 (nothing to do with the entry-level Porsche of the 1960s!). Because of an

LEFT 917, 1970

BELOW Ferdinand Piëch

agreement the company had with Volkswagen, the engine had to be air-cooled – which limited power but saved weight – which dictated a horizontally opposed layout, just like previous Porsche engines. However, this one had 12 cylinders and was, effectively two straight-sixes joined tog-ether. With a capacity of 4494cc, the engine produced an amazing 580bhp.

The 917 was first tested at Le Mans in March 1969 and reached speeds of up to 216mph on the straights. However, the test drivers had problems with the cars' handling, claiming that the chassis couldn't handle the engine's immense power and the car was very unstable. Although some tweaks were made, there was no time to do anything major before the Le Mans race in June. Two cars were entered by the factory, one driven by Rolf Stommelen and Kurt Ahrens, the second by Vic Elford and Richard Attwood. A third 917 was

entered by English businessman John Woolfe. Before the race, all the drivers agreed that the big Porsche was a handful to drive.

Tragically, in the first lap of the race Woolfe crashed, his car burst into flames and he was killed. Witnesses say he wasn't pushing the car particularly

LEFT 917 at Le Mans

hard and the loss of control was unexpected. The Stommelen/Ahrens car retired with clutch problems after 14 hours, but the Elford/Attwood team managed to make it into first place and held the lead overnight. With a 50-mile lead the next morning, they looked set to win until they too were forced out

with clutch failure. Still, they had set a new lap record of 145.411mph.

The following year, 1970, Porsche returned to Le Mans with a much-modified 917 that had a restyled body with a shorter, higher tail and a simpler front with none of the fins of the first car. The suspension and brakes were revised,

ABOVE 917 Daytona
24 hrs, 1970

and Richard Attwood. In 1971, Porsche 917s were in first and second place at Le Mans, with no less than 24 of the 51 entries being Porsches. The company gained massive publicity and sales rocketed.

The 917s were dominating in motorsport events around the world, not only Le Mans, and at the end of 1971 Porsche had been victorious at Monza, Spa, the Nürburgring and Zeltweg for three years in a row. Sadly, a change of rules for 1972 meant that a 3.0-litre limit to engine capacity, so the 5.0-litre 917s were no longer eligible to race in the Manufacturers' Championship. How-ever, the 917 continued to race in the American Can-Am series in the USA during 1972 and 1973. The cars became open-topped, had restyled bodies, and were equipped with twin turbochargers that boosted power to 1100bhp and gave the big Porsches a top speed of over 250mph. They were some of the fastest racing cars ever built.

too, while the engine was uprated to 4.9-litres and the transmission strengthened. The maximum power of the engine was now 600bhp. No less than seven 917s lined up at the start of the race, three of them factory cars under the new Gulf-Porsche banner with distinctive blue and orange livery. Porsches ended up taking first, second and third places, with the winner being the red Salsburg car driven by Hans Herrmann

911 success

THE 911 HAD LONG BEEN POPULAR in club racing but in 1973 the car moved up a league when a 911 RSR won the 24-hours of Daytona race, driven by Peter Gregg. This was the first time a 911 had won an international endurance event and demonstrated the capabilities of Porsche's new Carrera RS and RSR models.

These exciting new models were, in part, a reaction to the mega-expensive 917s that Porsche had been campaigning. It was, argued new Boss Fuhrmann, time to reel in the budgets and race something closer to production cars. By lightening the production 911 and fitting a more powerful engine, Porsche was able to produce a competitive machine that was relatively cheap to build and to buy – a far cry from the 917. The Carrera RS was essentially a

BELOW 911 Carrera RSR, Spa 1975

road car (although one that was successfully raced), but the RSR was a true racer and the first 911 to have an engine that produced 300bhp. Flared arches, wide wheels, uprated suspension and 917-derived brakes all combined to give a winning formula.

In 1973, the RSR proved successful on both sides of the Atlantic, with Peter Gregg winning the Trans-Am Drivers' Championship, as well as the Camel GT series. In Europe, several RSRs campaigned in the European GT Championship, with Clemens Schickentanz winning it for Porsche. What's

more, 3.0-litre Martini-sponsored cars that developed 330bhp raced in the Manufacturers' Championship, and in May 1973 one won the Targa Florio – Porsche's eleventh victory at the event. Even more impressive was a fourth place overall at Le Mans for a much-modified Martini RSR driven by Herbert Müller and Gijs van Lennep. The RSR was developed further in 1974 and helped cement the 911's position as one of the greatest sports cars ever, which gave a useful boost to sales, and the road-going 2.7 RS went on to be one of the most sought-after 911s.

BELOW 911 Carrera RSR, Nürburgring 1975

911 in
shape only

IN 1976, PORSCHE PRODUCED THE 935 to race in the new World Championship of Makes series. Regulations demanded that cars retained the basic silhouette and engine block of the production version, but just about everything else could be changed. That, of course, was just the sort of challenge Porsche's engineers loved.

The car was based loosely on a 911 Turbo, but heavily modified. For starters, it was fitted with coil springs instead of the usual torsion bars and had a cockpit-adjustable rear antiroll bar, while the body had a flatnose (which was later to find favour with buyers of road-going 911s), wide arches and a massive rear wing. Under that wing was a turbocharged 2808cc flat-six engine that produced over 600bhp. It was a formidable machine and, in that first year, won the World Championship of Makes. The following year, 1977, the engines had been refined and fitted with twin turbochargers to up power to 630bhp. This time Porsche took

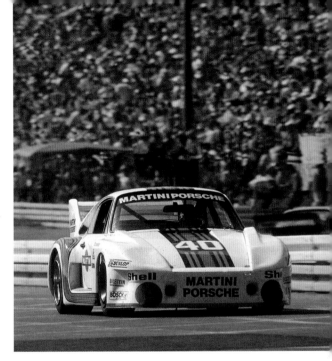

first and second places throughout the season.

However, there was more to come. The following year Porsche heavily modified the 935 with even larger wheelarch extensions covering massive wheels, and an extended tail under a large rear wing. This 935/78 was powered by a new 3.2-litre engine that featured liquid-cooling cylinder heads and twin KKK turbochargers. Its power output was no less than 845bhp. With its

ABOVE 935 'Moby Dick', Le Mans 1978

RIGHT Jürgen Barth and Hurley Haywood

BELOW RIGHT 936, Le Mans 1977

striking and aggressive shape, the car was dubbed 'Great White' by an German magazine, but that soon got changed to 'Moby Dick', after the fictional whale and the 935/78 has been known as that ever since.

Two 935/78s were built, but only one was raced. At Le Mans it finished in eighth place, held back by an oil leak. Nonetheless, everyone who drove it agreed that Moby Dick was a fantastic car, and it went on to become a legend.

Open champion – 936

AT THE SAME TIME THAT PORSCHE was building 935s, it was also developing an open-top racecar to compete in Group 6 competition. The 936 was loosely based on the 908 chassis of the 1960s, but fitted with modern bodywork that had been developed with the aid of a wind-tunnel. Its turbocharged,

2142cc flat-six engine produced
540bhp, and was fed air by a huge scoop
behind the driver's head.

For 1977, Porsche concentrated its
efforts on Le Mans, entering two 936s
into the event, driven by Jürgen Barth
and Hurley Haywood, and Jackie Ickx
and Henri Pescarolo. Despite struggling
with a seized cylinder, Barth drove his
car to victory, well ahead of the competitors. And in 1980 Derek Bell and
Jackie Ickx took an updated 936 to victory at Le Mans.

ABOVE 956 driven by Bell and Ickx, 1982

956 dominates Le Mans

BY THE EARLY 1980s PORSCHE WAS campaigning a new car at Le Mans. The Rothmans-sponsored 956 was the first Porsche race car to have a monocoque bodyshell and was designed to comply with new Group C regulations. The body shape was wind-tunnel-developed using ground-effect aerodynamics, in the same way that Formula One cars were going. Its mid-mounted, 2.6-litre, twin turbocharged flat-six engine developed 630bhp and could propel the car at speeds of up to 235mph.

At Le Mans in 1982 Derek Bell and Jackie Ickx drove a 956 to victory, while other 956s took second and third places. While the following year, the Porsches finished in the top eight places, with Vern Hschuppan, Hurley Haywood and Al Holbert driving the winning car. Porsche didn't enter Le Mans in 1983, but that didn't stop a privately entered 956 from winning, and again in 1984. In fact, the only thing that beat a 956 in 1985 was another Porsche – the essentially similar 962, which built primarily for racing in the USA.

BELOW 956 at Le Mans

Four-wheel-drive 959

THE 959 WAS A SUPERCAR WITH A difference – it competed not only in road races, but also in off-road rallies.

The 959 was, in part, developed to compete in the Paris-Dakar rally.

BELOW 959, Paris-Dakar Rally 1986

Initially, in 1984, the cars were simply modified 911s that had been fitted with four-wheel-drive transmission, yet one driven by Dominique Lemoyne and René Metge went on to win the event.

When the 959-proper arrived for the 1985 race, the cars were still fitted with 911 engines but were in other ways very advanced. Sadly, all three retired with mechanical problems. It wasn't until

1986 that a 959 would win the Paris-Dakar, but soon after that Group B rallying came to an end and so did Porsche's plans for rallying.

However, the news was somewhat better with the racing version of the 959, the 961. This was closely based on the production 959 and, in 1986, became the first four-wheel-drive car to compete at Le Mans. Driven by René

Metge and Claude Ballot-Lena, it suffered from mechanical problems but still finished seventh overall. The following year, Porsche's 959 hopes at Le Mans were dashed when the engine caught fire and the car had to retire.

ABOVE Derek Bell celebrates victory, 1987

Stunning GT1

PORSCHE CONTINUED TO HAVE successes at motorsport events around the world and then, in 1996, campaigned a new car in the GT class of Le Mans. This was the 911 GT1, of which a limited number were built as road cars for homologation purposes. Based very loosely on the 993-model 911, the GT1 was a stunning looking car, with a long, low bodyshell that bore some resemblance to a 911. However, the unique thing about the GT1 was that, unlike other 911s, it was mid-engined. This was partly to allow a more aerodynamic tail, and partly to give a better balance and therefore improved handling.

The engine itself was a 3164cc flat-six unit that was fully water-cooled and fed by twin KKK turbochargers. Maximum power was 600rpm, which no doubt helped the car to win its class at Le Mans that year, driven by Bob Wolleck, Thierry Boutsen and Hans Stuck.

Porsche heavily revamped the GT1 for its fiftieth anniversary in 1998. This time the restyled car had a lightweight carbonfibre chassis and even better aerodynamics. The two GT1s, driven by

Allan McNish, Stéphane Ortelli and Laurent Aiello, finished first and second overall at Le Mans, giving Porsche plenty to celebrate in its fiftieth year.

The GT1 was, to date, the last of the specially developed Porsche racecars, but GT1 and other racing Porsches continue to compete around the world in the hands of privateers. In addition to the cars mentioned here, all manner of production Porsches have been raced in various states of tune, from near-standard 924s to highly modified 911s. Whatever your budget, there's a Porsche race series to suit, and the competition is sure to be fast and furious.

OPPOSITE GT1 at Le Mans, 1997

LEFT Racing at Le Mans, 2004

BELOW Racing at Le Mans, 1998

Chapter 3

Porsches
through the years

HERE ARE JUST SOME of the most important and exciting road-going Porsches produced since 1950. It's not an exhaustive list – the company has produced literally hundreds of different variants (there are well over 50 for the 911 alone) – but you should find details of all the cars you're ever likely to spot, plus some you probably never will see!

BELOW 911 Carrera S, 2005

1953 **356 1500**

THE VERY FIRST 356s WERE HAND-built in an old sawmill in the Austrian town of Gmünd, and each one was slightly different. However, in 1950 production moved to Stuttgart in Germany and the cars became more standardised. Various models were produced over the years and the first, now known as Pre-A cars, were built from 1950 to 1955.

These pretty cars were offered in both closed coupe and open-top versions. The first had split windscreens, but in 1952 a single-piece screen was introduced, with a distinctive 'crease' down the centre.

Engine sizes of these early 356s varied from 1100cc to 1500cc. The torsion-bar suspension and rear-engined layout was to set the tone for the 911 which was to follow.

1964 **911**

THE FIRST OF THE 911s HAD A purity of line and a simplicity which makes them very desirable today. The monocoque body was penned by Ferdinand 'Butzi' Porsche and designed to be a two-plus-two with rear seats for children, plus space for luggage. In other words, it was to be a practical sports car.

The interior was also to set the style for 911s to follow. The dash featured five dials, with the tachometer right in front of the driver, and two smaller dials on each side. The low-backed front seats were simple affairs (although separate headrests could be added), while in the rear were a pair of small seats which could be folded down to create a luggage shelf – a feature that continued throughout the 911's development.

SPECIFICATION

Engine: Rear-mounted, air-cooled flat-six
Capacity: 1991cc
Compression ratio: 9.0:1
Maximum power: 130bhp at 6100rpm
Maximum torque: 173Nm at 4200rpm
Brakes: Front: 282mm discs; rear: 290mm discs
Suspension: Front: MacPherson struts with telescopic dampers and 19mm torsion bar springs; rear: Trailing wishbones with telescopic dampers and transverse 23mm torsion bar
Wheels & tyres: Front: 15x4.5J with 165HR tyres. Rear: 15x4.5J with 165HR tyres
Length: 4163mm
Width: 1610mm
Weight: 1080kg

1965 **912**

THE 911 WAS A FASTER, MORE complex and – crucially – more expensive car than the 356 which came before it. Porsche didn't want to lose potential sales to people who couldn't afford a 911, so it introduced the 912 in 1965.

This was essentially a 911 bodyshell fitted with the simpler four-cylinder, 1.6-litre engine from the last-of-the-line 356SC, which produced a modest 90bhp. As you'd expect the performance was reduced but still respectable for the period – 0-60mph took 11.6 seconds and the top speed was 115mph.

However, a happy side-effect of the smaller engine was that the 912 was some 130kg lighter than the 911, and because the weight-saving was at the back, the car was actually more balanced, thus making it handle better than the often tail-happy 911.

SPECIFICATION

Engine: Rear-mount, air-cooled flat-four
Capacity: 1582cc
Compression ratio: 8.5:1
Maximum power: 90bhp at 6100rpm
Maximum torque: 116Nm at 3500rpm
Brakes: Front: 282mm discs; rear: 290mm discs
Suspension: Front: MacPherson struts with telescopic dampers and torsion bar springs; rear: Trailing wishbones with telescopic dampers and transverse torsion bar
Wheels & tyres: Front: 15x4.5J with 165HR tyres. Rear: 15x4.5J with 165HR tyres
Length: 4163mm
Width: 1610mm
Weight: 935k

1968 **911S**

THE 911S (FOR SPORT) WAS A more powerful variant with an uprated and fuel-injected engine that pushed power to 170bhp – a high figure for 1968. It featured the now-classic Fuchs alloy wheels which were to go on to become a 911 trademark right up to 1989.

The 911S was an exciting car to drive – the extra power going through the rear wheels meant things could get exciting at times, and more than a few unsuspecting owners span the cars, sometimes with disastrous consequences.

Get it right, though, and the 911S rewarded you with a spirited and fun ride. After all, 911s were still relatively lightweight cars at this time, and 170bhp meant fast performance.

SPECIFICATION

Engine: Rear-mount, air-cooled flat-six
Capacity: 1991cc
Compression ratio: 9.9:1
Maximum power: 170bhp at 6800rpm
Maximum torque: 183Nm at 5500rpm
Brakes: Front: 282mm discs;
rear: 290mm discs
Suspension: Front: MacPherson struts with telescopic dampers and 19mm torsion bar springs; Rear: trailing wishbones with telescopic dampers and transverse torsion bar. Front and rear antiroll bars
Wheels & tyres: Front & rear: 15x6J with 185HR tyres
Length: 4163mm
Width: 1610mm
Weight: 995kg

1969 **911T**

BY 1969 THE 911 HAD AN ENGINE capacity of 2.2-litres and there were three models in the range; the 911E, the 911S, and the entry-level 911T.

While the other cars were fitted with fuel injection, to keeps costs down the 911T retained carburettors, which helped to make the 125bhp of power more useable than the rather revvy 911S. The Zenith carburettors also gave a nice induction roar, which was lost with the fuel-injected cars. So, despite being the cheapest 911 in the range, it was by no means an inferior car.

Steel wheels were standard equipment on the 911T at this time, but many buyers shunned these for the more attractive (and wider) Fuchs alloys, which were an extra-cost option.

SPECIFICATION

Engine: Rear-mounted, air-cooled flat-six

Capacity: 2195cc

Compression ratio: 8.6:1

Maximum power: 125bhp at 5800rpm

Maximum torque: 177Nm at 4200rpm

Brakes: Front: 282mm discs; rear: 290mm discs

Suspension: Front: MacPherson struts with telescopic dampers and torsion bar springs; Rear: Trailing wishbones with telescopic dampers and transverse torsion bar

Wheels & tyres: Front: 15x5.5J with 165HR tyres. Rear: 15x5.5J with 165HR tyres

Length: 4163mm

Width: 1610mm

Weight: 1020kg

1969
Porsche 914

PORSCHE DEVELOPED THE 914 IN conjunction with Volkswagen as an entry-level car to replace the 911-based 912.

The 914 was powered by a four-cylinder Volkswagen-designed engine that was mid-mounted to give an equal front/rear weight distribution for optimum handling. It was built in a separate factory by the coachbuilder Karmann and had distinctive, angular lines, quite unlike any other Porsche. The Targa

roof could be removed and stored in the luggage compartment to give open-top motoring.

While not a powerful car, the 912 handled extremely well, thanks to its mid-engine layout and well-thought-out, fully independent suspension set-up. However, it suffered throughout its life because of the Volkswagen connection – non-US cars even had a 'VW' badge on the back.

SPECIFICATION

Engine: Mid-mounted, air-cooled flat-four
Capacity: 1679cc
Compression ratio: 8.2:1
Maximum power: 80bhp
Maximum torque: 135Nm
Brakes: Front: 280mm discs; rear: 282mm discs
Suspension: Front: MacPherson struts with telescopic dampers and torsion bar springs; rear: trailing wishbones with telescopic dampers and coil springs. Front and rear antiroll bars
Wheels & tyres: Front: 15x4.5J with 165VR tyres. Rear: 15x4.5J with 165VR tyres
Length: 4050mm
Width: 1650mm
Weight: 970kg

1969
Porsche 914/6

THE 914 WAS ENDOWED WITH superb handling but, unfortunately the 80bhp four-cylinder engine didn't get the car the power it deserved.

Which is where the 914/6 came in. This was essentially the same car as the 914 but fitted with Porsche's own 2.0-litre flat-six engine, lifted from the contemporary 911T and fitted amidships in the 914/6.

This carburettor-equipped engine generated a useful 110bhp and this, combined with the already superb handling, transformed the 914 into a true sports car.

To help cope with the extra power, the 914/6 was given the front ventilated front disc brakes from the 911T, rather than the 914's Volkswagen-sourced items.

SPECIFICATION

Engine: Mid-mounted, air-cooled flat-six

Capacity: 1991cc

Compression ratio: 8.6:1

Maximum power: 110bhp at 5800rpm

Maximum torque: 156Nm at 4200rpm

Brakes: Front: 282mm discs;
rear: 282mm discs

Suspension: Front: MacPherson struts with telescopic dampers and torsion bar springs; rear: trailing wishbones with telescopic dampers and coil springs. Front and rear antiroll bars

Wheels & tyres: Front: 15x5.5J with 185VR tyres. Rear: 15x5.5J with 185VR tyres

Length: 4050mm

Width: 1650mm

Weight: 1020kg

1972-1973 **911 Carrera 2.7 RS**

THE 911 CARRERA 2.7 RS WAS developed as a homologation special to allow Porsche to compete in GT racing. It was developed from the 911S, with the engine increased in capacity to 2681cc to push power to 210bhp – a useful increase over the 911S's 190bhp.

However, the main performance gains were made by reducing weight. The roof, wings and bonnet were made of thinner steel, while the windscreen and rear quarter windows used thinner glass.

The rear arches were flared by 50mm each to accommodate wider 7-inch Fuchs alloys, and there was the option of a distinctive 'ducktail' spoiler. Also optional were large 'Carrera' side stripes in red, blue, black or green, with the Fuchs wheel centres colour-coded to match.

The suspension was tweaked with stiffer Koni dampers, uprated anti-roll bars and uprated mountings. Brakes remained standard 911S items.

SPECIFICATION

Engine: Rear-mounted, air-cooled flat-six
Capacity: 2681cc
Compression ratio: 8.5:1
Maximum power: 210bhp at 6300rpm
Maximum torque: 255Nm at 5100rpm
Brakes: Front: 282mm discs; rear: 290mm discs
Suspension: Front: MacPherson struts with telescopic Bilstein dampers and torsion bar springs; rear: trailing wishbones with telescopic dampers and transverse torsion bar. Front and rear antiroll bars
Wheels & tyres: Front: 15x6J with 185VR tyres. Rear: 15x7J with 215VR tyres
Length: 4163mm
Width: 1610mm
Weight: 975kg (Sport)

1975 **911 Turbo**

AT THE HEART OF THE FIRST 911 Turbo was a new 2994cc engine that was fed by a single KKK turbocharger, powered by the exhaust gases from both cylinder banks. Spinning at up to 100,000rpm, the turbocharger boosted engine power to 260bhp – an astonishing figure in the mid-1970s when turbos on road-going cars were still a novelty. The power was fed through a four-speed gearbox because Porsche felt its five-speed unit wouldn't cope and, besides, the engine's torque was such that a fifth gear wasn't necessary.

The Turbo's bodyshell was based on that of the contemporary 911, but fitted with much-extended wheel arches front and rear that gave the car a distinctive aggressive appearance. A whaletail rear spoiler was to become a trademark of the range-topping Porsche.

SPECIFICATION

Engine: Rear-mounted, air-cooled flat-six

Capacity: 2994cc

Compression ratio: 6.5:1

Maximum power: 260bhp at 5500rpm

Maximum torque: 343Nm at 4000rpm

Brakes: Front: 282mm discs; rear: 290mm discs

Suspension: Front: MacPherson struts with telescopic dampers and torsion bar springs; rear: trailing wishbones with telescopic dampers and transverse torsion bar. Front and rear antiroll bars

Wheels & tyres: Front: 15x7J with 185/70VR tyres. Rear: 15x8J with 215/60VR tyres

Length: 4491mm

Width: 1775mm

Weight: 1195kg

1976 **911 Carrera 3.0**

BY 1976 THE TOP OF THE RANGE 911 Carrera was fitted with a 3.0-litre, fuel-injected engine that produced 200bhp. This engine would continue, with only minor changes, to power the 911 right up until 1989.

To meet US regulations, the 911 was now fitted with impact-absorbing bumpers with distinctive rubber bel-

lows at each side. It also had large, square door mirrors which were electrically operated and dubbed 'elephant ears'. An option was a large 'whaletail' spoiler, which was similar to that fitted to the 911 Turbo and helped to improve stability at high-speed.

A novel new feature of the Carrera 3.0 was an automatic heating system, with a controller between the front seats. This was an attempt to tame the 911's temperamental cabin heat.

SPECIFICATION

Engine: Rear-mounted, air-cooled flat-six
Capacity: 2994cc
Compression ratio: 8.5:1
Maximum power: 200bhp at 6000rpm
Maximum torque: 255Nm at 4200rpm
Brakes: Front: 282mm discs; rear: 290mm discs
Suspension: Front: MacPherson struts with telescopic dampers and torsion bar springs; rear: trailing wishbones with telescopic dampers and transverse torsion bar. Front and rear antiroll bars
Wheels & tyres: Front: 15x6J with 185VR tyres. Rear: 15x7J with 215VR tyres
Length: 4291mm
Width: 1610mm
Weight: 1093kg

1976 **924**

THE 924 WAS PORSCHE'S NEW entry-level car, developed partly in conjunction with Volkswagen, and for a time it was almost badged a VW.

It was a departure for Porsche in that it had a front-mounted, water-cooled four-cylinder engine, linked to a rear-mounted gearbox driving the back wheels. The engine itself was a 2.0-litre Audi unit which Porsche modified to give more power. The front engine/rear transmission layout gave a balanced weight distribution to optimise the handling.

The 924 was a good-looking car with its smooth lines and fashionable pop-up headlamps. It was also very practical with its small rear seats and an opening rear hatch. Despite not being a high performer, the 924 was a great sales success, winning Porsche many new customers.

SPECIFICATION

Engine: Front-mounted, water-cooled straight-four

Capacity: 1984cc

Compression ratio: 9.3:1

Maximum power: 125bhp at 5800rpm

Maximum torque: 165Nm at 3500rpm

Brakes: Front: 256.5mm discs; rear: 228.6mm drums

Suspension: Front: MacPherson struts with telescopic dampers and coil springs; rear: trailing wishbones with telescopic dampers and transverse torsion basr. Optional front and rear antiroll bars

Wheels & tyres: Front: 14x5.5J with 165HR14 tyres. Rear: 14x5.5J with 165HR14 tyres

Length: 4213mm

Width: 1676mm

Weight: 1080kg

1978 **928**

THE 928 WAS DEVELOPED TO replace the 911 but it never did. It was quite a different car, with a large, water-cooled V8 engine mounted at the front, driving the back wheels via a rear-mounted gearbox, to give an even weight distribution.

The 928 was a large car and boasted spaceship-like lines that seemed very futuristic in the mid-1970s, with exposed pop-up headlamps and lots of glass, including a lifting hatchback to give access to the luggage area.

It was the same story inside, with a luxurious and modern interior with an instrument pod that moved in conjunction with the steering column. The back seats cocooned small children in comfort, while in the front there was plenty of space for two adults to stretch out and enjoy long journeys.

Even though the 928 wasn't the 911 replacement Porsche had hoped for, it was a great car in its own right and gained many fans over the years.

SPECIFICATION

Engine: Front-mounted, water-cooled V8
Compression ratio: 8.5:1
Maximum power: 240bhp at 5500rpm
Maximum torque: 348Nm at 3600rpm
Brakes: Front: 282mm discs; rear: 289.5mm drums
Suspension: Front: Double wishbones with telescopic dampers and coil springs; rear: upper transverse links, lower trailing arms with telescopic dampers. Front and rear antiroll bars
Wheels & tyres: Front: 16x7.0J with 225HR50/14 tyres. Rear: 16x7.0J with 225HR50/14 tyres
Length: 4445mm
Width: 1836mm
Weight: 1468kg

1978 **911SC**

IN 1978 PORSCHE STREAMLINED its 911 model range with the introduction of the SC – it was the only normally aspirated 911 you could buy, which made life easier after the confusing range of models offered in previous years.

It had a tough 3.0-litre, fuel-injected engine that, in initial form, produced 180bhp and went through a 915 five-speed gearbox, or a rarely selected optional Sportomatic transmission that dispensed with the clutch pedal.

A popular option for the SC was the Sport package. This consisted of a whaletail rear spoiler, a rubber extension to the front spoiler, Bilstein gas dampers, 16-inch Fuchs wheels and sports seats.

In 1981, the power of the engine rose to 204bhp y raising the compression ratio to 9.8:1 changing the camshaft timing and tweaking the fuel injection system. The model was replaced by the Carrera 3.2 after 1983.

SPECIFICATION

Capacity: 2994cc
Compression ratio: 8.5:1
Maximum power: 180 at 5500rpm
Maximum torque: 265Nm at 4300rpm
Brakes: Front: 287mm discs; rear: 295mm discs. Servo assisted
Wheels & tyres: Front: 15x6J with 185/70VR tyres. Rear: 15x7J with 215/60VR tyres (16inch rims optional).
Length: 4291mm
Width: 1626mm
Weight: 1160kg (coupé)

1979 **924 Turbo**

DESPITE BEING A SALES SUCCESS, the 924 was criticised from the day it was launched for being underpowered. The obvious solution for Porsche, following the success of the 911 Turbo was to come up with a turbocharged version of its entry-level car.

The engine was modified and fitted with a KKK K26 turbocharger and an external oil cooler. This gave a respectable output of 170bhp, which went through a racing-style dogleg gearbox.

Brakes were uprated, too, with larger discs at the front, and rear discs in place of the standard car's drums.

Externally, the Turbo was treated to air vents in the nose, a NACA bonnet duct, a polyurethane rear spoiler, while two-tone paint was a popular option. Wheels were new five-stud, multispoke items.

SPECIFICATION

Engine: Front-mounted, water-cooled straight-four

Capacity: 1984cc

Compression ratio: 7.5:1

Maximum power: 125bhp at 5800rpm

Maximum torque: 245Nm at 3500rpm

Brakes: Front: 282mm discs; rear: 289mm discs

Suspension: Front: MacPherson struts with telescopic dampers and coil springs; rear: trailing wishbones with telescopic dampers and transverse torsion basr. Optional front and rear antiroll bars

Wheels & tyres: Front: 15x6J with 185HR70/15 tyres. Rear: 15x6J with 185HR70/15 tyres

Length: 4213mm

Width: 1676mm

Weight: 1180kg

1983 **944**

AT FIRST SIGHT, THE 944 WAS JUST a facelifted 924 but, in fact, it was much more than that. The front and rear wheel arches were flared out to give the car a much more aggressive demeanour, and to cover the larger wheels.

However, the big news was that the 944 had a new engine to replace the underpowered Volkswagen-derived unit of the 924. The 2.5-litre Porsche-designed engine had balance-shafts to compensate for the inherent imbalance of the four-cylinders and, with an out-

put of 163bhp it put paid to criticisms that the original 924 was an underpowered VW.

The front-mounted engine and rear gearbox gave a good weight distribution which, combined with revised suspension, ensured that the 944 handled superbly.

The 944 received a number of updates until it was replaced by the 968 in 1989.

SPECIFICATION

Capacity: 2479cc
Compression ratio: 10.6:1
Maximum power: 163bhp at 5800rpm
Maximum torque: 205Nm at 3000rpm
Brakes: Front: 282mm discs; rear: 289mm discs. Servo assisted
Wheels & tyres: Front: 15x7J with 185/70VR15 tyres. Rear: 15x8J with 215/60VR tyres
Length: 4213mm
Width: 1735mm
Weight: 1180kg

1984 **911 Carrera 3.2**

THE 1984 911 CARRERA 3.2 HAD essentially the same galvanised body as the outgoing SC, albeit with a new front spoiler with integral fog-lamps. The interior was also very similar to that of the SC, with just revised seat fabrics and trims.

The engine, on the other hand, was claimed by Porsche to be 80 per cent new, although based on the SC's 3.0-litre unit. Capacity rose to 3164cc but the Carrera's main innovation was its Bosch Motronic 2 engine management system. This was the first production 911 to feature an ECU to control the ignition and fuel systems, and the power output was 231bhp.

Initially, the Carrera 3.2 was offered with the same 915 gearbox as the SC. However, in 1987 the car was treated to the new Getrag G50 gearbox which offered smoother changes and a shorter, more modern-looking, gearlever.

SPECIFICATION

Capacity: 3164cc
Compression ratio: 10.3:1
Maximum power: 231bhp at 5900rpm
Maximum torque: 284Nm at 4800rpm
Brakes: Front: 304mm discs; rear: 309mm discs. Servo assisted
Wheels & tyres: Front: 15x7J with 195/65VR tyres. Rear: 15x8J with 215/60VR tyres (16inch rims optional).
Length: 4291mm
Width: 1650mm
Weight: 1210kg (coupé)

1985 **944 Turbo**

THE 944 WAS TRULY A GREAT improvement on the 924, but Porsche turned it into a true budget-priced supercar when it introduced the 944 Turbo. Not that the car was cheap – it was about the same price as a contemporary 911 – but the performance was phenomenal for the money.

Using essentially the same engine as the 944, a single KKK K26 turbocharger boosted power to 220bhp. This gave the 944 Turbo a 0-60mph time of just 5.9 seconds, with a maximum speed of 162mph.

Handling and brakes were uprated to cope with the extra power, the latter with larger discs and four-piston calipers.

The 944 Turbo was treated to a new front end with an integral polyurethane bumper (which was later to be used on all the 944 range). At the back was an enlarged tailgate spoiler, plus a distinctive under-spoiler.

Inside was an all-new oval-shaped dash that served to distance the Turbo from its 924 roots. The same dash went on to be standard fitment across the whole range.

The engine was uprated to 250bhp in 1988 and the model was discontinued in 1991.

SPECIFICATION

Capacity: 2479cc

Compression ratio: 8.0:1

Maximum power: 220bhp at 5800rpm

Maximum torque: 330Nm at 3500rpm

Brakes: Front: 282mm discs; rear: 289mm discs. Servo assisted

Wheels & tyres: Front: 16x7J with 205/55VR16 tyres. Rear: 16x8J with 225/50VR/16 tyres

Length: 4230mm

Width: 1735mm

Weight: 1350kg

1986 **959**

DEVELOPED IN THE MID-EIGHTIES as an homologation special to enable Porsche to compete in Gruppe B motorsport, the 959 became one of the most technologically advanced – and fastest – cars ever built.

Based on a 911, the 959 had carbonfibre body panels, sophisticated four-wheel-drive, six-speed gearbox, active suspension, magnesium-alloy wheels with tyre-pressure sensors, run-flat tyres, and stunningly styled lines.

The engine was an all-aluminium unit that was essentially air-cooled, but with water-cooled cylinder heads. Two sequential turbochargers and twin intercoolers helped it to produce no less than 450bhp.

With power like this going to all four wheels, the 959 could rocket to 62mph in just 3.7 seconds, and go on to a top speed of 197mph. Figures that few cars have beaten to this day.

It is believed that just 292 road-going 959s were built, making it a rare and sought-after machine.

SPECIFICATION

Capacity: 2847cc
Compression ratio: 8.3:1
Maximum power: 450bhp at 6500rpm
Maximum torque: 500Nm at 5500rpm
Brakes: Front: 322mm discs; rear: 308mm discs. Servo assisted
Wheels & tyres: Front: 17x8J with 235/45VR17 tyres. Rear: 17x10J with 255/40VR17 tyres
Length: 4260mm
Width: 1840mm
Weight: 1650kg

1986 **911 Turbo SE**

THE PORSCHE 935 RACECARS OF the late 1970s onwards had wings that swept down in line with the bonnet, to aid aerodynamics. Customers began asking for these on road-going 911s so Porsche gave them the 911 Turbo SE.

As well as the slantnose and pop-up headlamps, extended sills ran down the sides of the car and met with rear wings that featured massive air intakes with distinctive horizontal strakes. Claimed to vent air to the rear brakes, these were more cosmetic than anything, but did serve to give the SE an aggressive appearance. At the front, there was a deeper spoiler with an additional, centre oil cooler behind.

The 911 Turbo SE had a maximum output of 330bhp – 30bhp up on the standard Turbo. This was achieved by means of a larger KKK turbocharger, higher-lift camshafts, higher boost pressure, larger intercooler and a sports exhaust system with four outlets.

SPECIFICATION

Capacity: 3299cc
Compression ratio: 7.0:1
Maximum power: 330bhp at 5500rpm
Maximum torque: 432Nm at 4000rpm
Brakes: Front: 304mm discs; rear:309mm discs
Wheels & tyres: Front: 16x7J with 205/55VR tyres. Rear: 16x9J with 245/45VR tyres
Length: 4491mm
Width: 1775mm
Weight: 1335kg

1989 **Speedster**

THE SPEEDSTER WAS INSPIRED BY the 356 Speedster of the 1950s and based on the 911 3.2 Carrera.

It had a more steeply raked windscreen than the standard 911 in a lightweight aluminium frame. The hood was lower and sat atop smaller, frameless side windows. When the hood was lowered it was stored under a twin-humped plastic panel.

The majority of the 2065 Speedsters built had the wide Turbo-Look front and rear wings, although a few were built with the narrow body, while a handful were Slant-Noses.

Specification was simple with manually operated windows, seats and heater. There were no rear seats because the area was taken up by the hood cover, although there was some storage space below.

SPECIFICATION

Capacity: 3164cc

Compression ratio: 10.3:1

Maximum power: 231bhp at 5900rpm

Maximum torque: 284Nm at 4800rpm

Brakes: Front: 304mm discs; rear: 309mm discs. Servo assisted

Suspension: Front: Twin longitudinal torsion-bar springs, anti-roll bar, Boge dampers; Rear: Semi-trailing arms with torsion-bar springs, anti-roll bar, Boge dampers

Wheels & tyres: Front: 15x7J with 195/65VR tyres. Rear: 15x8J with 215/60VR tyres (16inch rims optional).
In 1989: Front: 16x6J with 205/55VR tyres. Rear: 16x8J with 225/50VR tyres

Length: 4291mm

Width: 1650mm

Weight: 1210kg

1989 **911 Carrera 4**

CODENAMED 964, THIS WAS THE first major revamp of the 911, and was claimed to be 87 percent new.

The big news was a four-wheel-drive transmission system helped eliminate the 911's previously rather wayward handling, and also proved to buyers that the car was now bang up to date.

Also new was conventional coil spring suspension, in place of the quirky torsion bars, ABS brakes, and a 3.6-litre engine with twin spark plugs per cylinder.

The body was updated with integrated deformable bumpers and a clever retractable spoiler. This lifted up when the car reached 50mph, and then dropped down again at a little over walking pace. The raised tail gave much-needed downforce at speed and also improved engine cooling.

The Carrera 4 was followed in 1990 by a rear-wheel-drive Carrera 2, and the model continued until 1993.

SPECIFICATION

Capacity: 3600cc

Compression ratio: 10.3:1

Maximum power: 250bhp at 6100rpm

Maximum torque: 310Nm at 4800rpm

Brakes: Front: 298mm discs; rear: 299mm discs. Servo assisted with ABS

Wheels & tyres: Front: 16x6J with 205/55ZR16 tyres. Rear: 16x8J with 225/50ZR16 tyres (17-inch rims optional)

Length: 4250mm

Width: 1650mm

Weight: 1450kg (coupé)

1990 **911 Turbo**

THE 911 TURBO REAPPEARED IN A new form in 1990, using the revised 964 bodyshell with its integrated bumpers but endowed with extended front and rear arches, and a 'teatray' fixed rear spoiler to give the familiar Turbo appearance.

The 3.3-litre engine came from the previous model but was updated with new, more efficient, inlet and exhaust systems, the latter with dual outlets. In addition, the Bosch Motronic engine management system was revised and the intercooler enlarged. The upshot of all this was an increase in power from 300bhp to 320bhp.

To ensure the Turbo stopped as well as it went, it was equipped with the ABS system from the Carrera 2, but with larger discs. Suspension, too, was based on that of the Carrera, but uprated with stiffer springs and dampers.

In 1992 the 964-model 911 Turbo was updated with a more powerful 3.6-litre engine, before the variant was discontinued in 1993.

SPECIFICATION

Capacity: 3299cc
Compression ratio: 7.0:1
Maximum power: 320bhp at 5750rpm
Maximum torque: 450Nm at 4500rpm
Brakes: Front: 322mm discs; rear: 299mm discs. Servo assisted with ABS
Wheels & tyres: Front: 17x7J with 205/50ZR17 tyres. Rear: 17x9J with 255/45ZR17 tyres
Length: 4250mm
Width: 1775mm
Weight: 1470kg

1991 **911 Carrera 2 RS**

A WORTHY SUCCESSOR TO THE 1973 RS, this was a lightweight version of the 964-model Carrera 2. Around 120kg was shaved from the car by deleting 'luxuries' such as a sunroof, electric windows, electric mirrors, rear seats, door pockets, and much of the sound insulation, while the side windows were made of thinner glass. Seats were lightweight Recaros and there were simple pull-straps on the doors.

The engine was given a 10bhp power boost to 260bhp by tweaking the engine management system, while a lightweight, solid flywheel helped the engine to be more responsive and was linked to a harder clutch plate. The power went through a G50 five-speed gearbox modified with revised ratios, stronger synchromeshes, shorter gearlever and a limited slip differential.

The suspension was lowered by 40mm and enhanced by rigid rear swing arms, larger antiroll bars, front strutbrace, and stiffer springs and dampers. The brakes were uprated, too.

SPECIFICATION

Capacity: 3600cc
Compression ratio: 10.3:1
Maximum power: 260bhp at 6100rpm
Maximum torque: 310Nm at 4800rpm
Brakes: Front: 322mm discs; rear: 299mm discs. Servo assisted with ABS
Wheels & tyres: Front: 17x7.5J with 205/50ZR17 tyres. Rear: 17x9J with 255/40ZR17 tyres
Length: 4250mm
Width: 1650mm
Weight: 1230kg (Sport)

1991 **968**

THE 944 WENT ON TO RECEIVE A major revamp and became the 968 in 1991. The new car's 924 parentage remained very obvious, especially amidships, but was treated to a smart new front with more shapely wings and exposed flip-up headlamps, similar to those of the 928. The rear end, too, was smoothed out and given a new-style spoiler. Teardrop mirrors and Cup wheels completed the transformation.

However, it was not just cosmetic. The 968's 3.0-litre engine was reworked to give more power and torque, from lower revs. And the power went through a new six-speed gearbox which, as before, was mounted at the rear of the car, between the wheels. The interior remained similar to that of the last 944, but received minor updates.

A ClubSport version offered a stripped-out interior and lower, firmer suspension, while the Sport was a compromise between the ClubSport and the standard, fully trimmed car. The model continued until 1993.

SPECIFICATION

Capacity: 2990cc
Compression ratio: 11.0:1
Maximum power: 240bhp at 6200rpm
Maximum torque: 305Nm at 4100rpm
Brakes: Front: 297mm discs; rear: 300mm discs. Servo assisted
Wheels & tyres: Front: 16x7J with 205/50ZR16 tyres. Rear: 16x8J with 225/40ZR/16 tyres
Length: 4320mm
Width: 1735mm
Weight: 1370kg

1993
911 Carrera

FOR THE 993-MODEL, PORSCHE took the 911 bodyshell and gave it a bold new identity, but without losing the classic profile – the new car was still instantly recognisable for what it was.

At the front, the wings became lower and more shapely and had tipped back headlamps, while the bumper was more integrated. Out back, the wings curved out in a sensuous manner and blended into a more integral bumper and restyled lights and central reflector. The retractable rear spoiler was similar to that of the 964, but was more flush-fitting when lowered. Other visual changes included flusher window frames, new exterior door handles and redesigned windscreen wipers.

The 3.6-litre was updated and fitted with hydraulic tappets, and was linked to a new six-speed gearbox. An all-new multi-link rear suspension system had parallel wishbones attached to a sturdy aluminium subframe.

A four-wheel-drive Carrera 4 followed in 1994.

SPECIFICATION

Capacity: 3600cc

Compression ratio: 11.3:1

Maximum power: 272bhp at 6000rpm (285bhp from 1996)

Maximum torque: 330Nm at 5000rpm (340Nm from 1996)

Brakes: Front: 304mm discs; rear: 299mm discs. Servo assisted with ABS

Wheels & tyres: Front: 16x7J with 205/55ZR16 tyres. Rear: 16x9J with 245/45ZR16 tyres (17-inch rims optional)

Length: 4245mm

Width: 1735mm

Weight: 1370kg (coupé)

1995 **GT2**

A ROAD-GOING VERSION OF THE GT2 race car, this was basically a 993-model Turbo, but to save weight out went all the unnecessary luxuries. Electric windows and seats, air-conditioning, much of the sound insulation, sunroof, and interior door furniture. In it place came thinner glass, aluminium bonnet and doors.

The power came from same twin-turbo engine from the Turbo, albeit tweaked to produce 430bhp, compared with the standard car's 408bhp. However, it was directed to the rear wheels only to save weight and to create a purer track car.

The bodywork was treated to huge plastic wheelarch extensions with visible bolts, while at the front, a deep lip spoiler had distinctive turned up ends. The rear had a huge adjustable wing and side inlets that forced air to the engine.

With a claimed 0-62mph time of 4.4 seconds (reducing to 3.1 in the case of the full-race version) and a top speed of 189mph the GT2 was very fast, by anyone's standards.

SPECIFICATION

Capacity: 3600cc

Compression ratio: 8.0:1

Maximum power: 430bhp at 5750rpm

Maximum torque: 540Nm at 4500rpm

Brakes: Front: 322mm discs; rear: 322mm discs. Servo assisted with ABS

Wheels & tyres: Front: 18x9J with 235/40ZR18 tyres. Rear: 18x11J with 285/35ZR18 tyres

Length: 4245mm

Width: 1855mm

Weight: 1290kg

1996 **911 Turbo**

GIVING THE ALREADY GOOD -looking 993 the wide-body Turbo treatment was a surefire recipe for success. The rear arches were stretched by 30mm each, while the were enlarged downwards to make room for three large air-intakes in the nose, and to improve aerodynamics at the back. Also at the rear the teatray spoiler now wrapped itself over the engine cover.

The engine was essentially the 3.6-litre unit from the normally aspirated 911 but with a lower compression ratio two KKK K16 turbochargers rather than one to reduce turbo-lag and give 408bhp of power. This power was fed to all four wheels, using the transmission from the Carrera 4, thus making the Turbo safer and more driveable than ever.

The brakes were suitably uprated from those in the Carrera and featured bright-red four-piston calipers. The Turbo's wheels had hollow spokes to save weight and were shaped so that they actually sucked cooling air onto the brakes behind.

The 993-model Turbo remained in production until 1998.

SPECIFICATION

Capacity: 3600cc

Compression ratio: 8.0:1

Maximum power: 408bhp at 5750rpm

Maximum torque: 540Nm at 4500rpm

Brakes: Front: 322mm discs; rear: 322mm discs. Servo assisted with ABS

Wheels & tyres: Front: 18x8J with 225/40ZR18 tyres. **Rear:** 18x10J with 285/30ZR18 tyres

Length: 4245mm

Width: 1795mm

Weight: 1575kg

1997 **Boxster**

DEVELOPED IN CONJUNCTION with the 996-model 911, the Boxster was an entry-level model to replace the ageing 968. It was an all-new design that carried nothing over from the previous Porsche.

The Boxster was an open-topped car with a mid-mounted, water-cooled flat-six engine that was similar to the larger unit in the 996. The 2.5-litre engine had four valves per cylinder, VarioCam vari-able valve timing and Bosch Motronic engine management. The engine was totally hidden from view – all the owner could see was filler caps for the oil and coolant.

Strictly a two-seater, the cockpit was modern and well-equipped, with an electrically operated hood that folded neatly away when open. A hard-top was an optional extra. Luggage could be stored in compartments at the front and back of the car.

The Boxster was updated with a more powerful 2.7-litre engine and other refinements in 1999, followed by a new model in 2005.

SPECIFICATION

Capacity: 2480cc
Compression ratio: 11.0:1
Maximum power: 204bhp at 6000rpm
Maximum torque: 244Nm at 4500rpm
Brakes: Front: 304mm discs; rear: 299mm discs. Servo assisted with ABS
Wheels & tyres: Front: 16x6J with 205/50ZR16 tyres. Rear: 16x7J with 225/40ZR16 tyres (17-inch rims optional)
Length: 4133mm
Width: 1740mm
Weight: 1250kg

1997 **911 Carrera**

THE ALL-NEW 911 HAD, FOR THE first time, a water-cooled engine. This new 3.4-litre engine boasted four valves per cylinder (a first for a production 911) and an output of 300bhp. Power went through a six-speed gearbox or an optional five-speed Tiptronic automatic transmission, with fingertip controls on the steering wheel.

The body was larger and more aerodynamic than the old 911, The windscreen was more steeply raked, the air-intake had disappeared from the top of the bonnet, as had the front quarter lights, and there were distinctively shaped headlamps with integral orange indicators.

Inside, out went the distinctive but quirky dash design and in its place came a modern, easy to use layout. The trademark five dials – with the rev counter central – remained, but they were now neatly overlapped.

The Carrera was joined by a four-wheel-drive Carrera 4 in 1998. The range continued until 2005, when the 997-model 911 replaced it.

SPECIFICATION

Capacity: 3387cc
Compression ratio: 11.3:1
Maximum power: 300bhp at 6800rpm
Maximum torque: 350Nm at 4600rpm
Brakes: Front: 318mm discs; rear: 299mm discs. Servo assisted with ABS
Wheels & tyres: Front: 17x7J with 205/50ZR17 tyres. Rear: 17x9J with 255/40ZR17 tyres (18-inch rims optional)
Length: 4430mm
Width: 1765mm
Weight: 1320kg (coupé)

1999 **GT3**

A RACE-INSPIRED, LIGHTWEIGHT
996-model 911, the GT3 had a 3600cc
engine combining the bottom end of
the GT1 racecar unit with the water-
cooled and multi-valve heads from the
996 Carrera. To save weight and to give
racecar handling, the GT3 was rear-
wheel-drive using a six-speed gearbox.

The GT3 was distinguished by a large
rear spoiler and a deeper front spoiler

with restyled air intakes, while sill
extensions gave the car a lower stance.

Inside, there were no rear seats, while
the ClubSport was stripped right back
to basics with manual window winders,
no air-conditioning or radio, while full
harnesses, fire extinguisher and a
rollcage meant the car was track-ready.

The Comfort version was more like a
conventional 911 inside, although air-
conditioning, leather upholstery and a
centre console were all extra, as were
most other 911 options.

A total of 1890 GT3s were built in
1999 and 2000. It was followed by a new
version in 2003.

SPECIFICATION

Capacity: 3600cc
Compression ratio: 11.7:1
Maximum power: 360bhp at 6300rpm
Maximum torque: 370Nm at 5100rpm
Brakes: Front: 330mm discs; rear: 330mm
discs. Servo assisted with ABS
Wheels & tyres: Front: 18x8J with
225/40ZR18 tyres. Rear: 18x10J with
285/30ZR18 tyres
Length: 4430mm
Width: 1765mm
Weight: 1350kg

1999 **Boxster S**

THE ORIGINAL BOXSTER WAS A very capable car, with its mid-mounted engine and excellent suspension. So capable, in fact, that many felt it deserved more power so that the chassis could be fully exploited.

They got their wish when the Boxster S was launched. This combined the Boxster bodyshell with a larger 3.2-litre version of the flat-six engine that produced 252bhp – a useful 48bhp increase on the 2.5-litre version. This was enough to propel the S to 62mph in just 5.9 seconds and go on to a top speed of 162mph. The Boxster had really come of age with the S variant.

Externally, there was little to distinguish the S from the standard car. It had a lined hood, which reduced noise and 17-inch wheels with a new design were standard (18-inch ones were optional).

Red-painted calipers denoted the uprate brakes which were based on 911 items.

The Boxster S received a power upgrade to 260bhp in 2002, plus other improvements. A new model arrived in 2005.

SPECIFICATION

Capacity: 3179cc

Compression ratio: 11.2:1

Maximum power: 252bhp at 6250rpm

Maximum torque: 305Nm at 4500rpm

Brakes: Front: 318mm discs; rear: 299mm discs. Servo assisted with ABS

Wheels & tyres: Front: 17x7J with 205/50ZR17 tyres. Rear: 17x8.5J with 225/40ZR17 tyres (18-inch rims optional)

Length: 4133mm

Width: 1740mm

Weight: 1295kg

2000 **911 Turbo**

The 996-model 911 Turbo had widened rear arches with large air intakes, while a deeper front spoiler housed three more intakes. At the back was a fixed spoiler with a section that raised at speed. A set of 18-inch wheels (a full 11 inches wide at the back) completed the aggressive look.

Power came from a 3600cc engine that produced 420bhp while the maximum torque of 560Nm was available from 2700 to 4600rpm. The unit was derived from the normally aspired 996 and fitted with twin KKK K17 turbochargers. Power went to all four wheels using basically the same transmission as the Carrera 4.

Brakes were uprated, while an option were ceramic brake discs in place of the more usual cast-iron ones. These were made from carbon-reinforced silicon carbide.

With a 0-62mph time of just 4.2 seconds and a top speed of 189mph, the 996-model 911 Turbo was hard to beat, especially because the power and handling were so user friendly. Here was a supercar anyone could drive.

SPECIFICATION

Capacity: 3600cc
Compression ratio: 9.4:1
Maximum power: 420bhp at 6000rpm
Maximum torque: 560Nm at 2700 to 4600rpm
Brakes: Front: 330mm discs; rear: 330mm discs. Servo assisted with ABS
Wheels & tyres: Front: 18x8J with 225/40ZR18 tyres. Rear: 18x11J with 295/30ZR18 tyres
Length: 4435mm
Width: 1830mm
Weight: 1540kg (coupé)

2001
Carrera 4S

THE NEW CARRERA 4S COMBINED the wide Turbo bodyshell with the drivetrain from the standard Carrera 4. The Turbo's front and rear bumpers, with their intakes, remained, but the wide rear wings lacked any air intakes (they weren't required for the normally aspirated engine) and, instead of the Turbo's part-fixed rear spoiler, the 4S had the standard car's fully retractable item.

At the back was a full-width rear reflector which harked back to the style of older 911s – a feature that went down well with die-hard enthusiasts.

However, there was more to the Carrera 4S than just good looks. The uprated suspension was based on that of the Turbo, so the car was 10mm lower than the standard Carrera. The brakes, too, came straight from the 911 Turbo and gave phenomenal stopping performance. The wheels were also the 18-inch Turbo items.

The Carrera 4S continued in production until 2005.

SPECIFICATION

Capacity: 3596cc

Compression ratio: 11.3:1

Maximum power: 320bhp at 6800rpm

Maximum torque: 370Nm at 4250rpm

Brakes: Front: 330mm discs; rear: 330mm discs. Servo assisted with ABS

Wheels & tyres: Front: 18x8J with 225/40ZR18 tyres. Rear: 18x11J with 295/30ZR18 tyres

Length: 4435mm

Width: 1830mm

Weight: 1495kg (coupé)

2001 **GT2**

THE MOST EXTREME 996 VARIANT, the GT2 used basically the same engine as the 911 Turbo, but with larger turbochargers and other tweaks which upped maximum power to 460bhp. A crucial difference to the Turbo was that all this power went through the rear wheels only and there was no PSM (Porsche Stability Management). With a top speed of 192mph and a 0-62mph-time of 4.0 seconds, the GT2 was not for the faint-hearted.

The suspension was lowered and uprated and ceramic brake discs (with distinctive yellow calipers) were standard equipment.

The bodyshell was that of the 911 Turbo, with the same wide rear wings with air intakes in each side. However, at the front the air intakes were dissected by a horizontal bar, while an additional splitter increased downforce. At the back, downforce was further increased by a large, fixed spoiler.

In 2004 the GT2's engine was uprated to 483bhp and the aerodynamics were improved.

SPECIFICATION

Capacity: 3600cc
Compression ratio: 9.4:1
Maximum power: 462bhp at 5700rpm
Maximum torque: 620Nm at 3500 to 4500rpm
Brakes: Front: 350mm discs; rear: 350mm discs. Servo assisted with ABS
Wheels & tyres: Front: 18x8.5J with 235/40ZR18 tyres. Rear: 18x12J with 315/30ZR18 tyres
Length: 4435mm
Width: 1830mm
Weight: 1440kg

2003 Cayenne

The Cayenne marked a radical departure for Porsche in that it was the first time the company had built anything other than a sports car. However, Porsche's engineers used its expertise to ensure that the big four-by-four handled better than the opposition, both on and off road.

This entry-level Cayenne was fitted with an all-new front-mounted V6 engine that produced 250bhp, enough to propel the heavy SUV to 62mph in

9.1 seconds and on to a top speed of 133mph.

Power went through either a six-speed manual gearbox which had Porsche Drive Off Assistant, which made it easier to start on a hill by automatically controlling the brakes. An six-speed Tiptronic automatic transmission was optional.

The four-wheel-drive system was highly sophisticated, with Porsche Traction Management which controlled how much power went to the front or rear. Under normal conditions the ratio was 63 percent rear and 38 percent front, but this could change to as much as 100 percent front or rear if required.

SPECIFICATION

Capacity: 3189cc

Compression ratio: 11.5:1

Maximum power: 250bhp at 6000rpm

Maximum torque: 310Nm at 2500-5500rpm

Brakes: Front: 330mm discs; rear: 330mm discs. Servo assisted with ABS

Wheels & tyres: Front: 17x7.5J with 235/65R17 tyres. Rear: 17x7.5J with 235/65R17 tyres (18-, 19- and 20-inch rims optional)

Length: 4782mm

Width: 1928mm

Weight: 2160kg

2003 **Cayenne Turbo S**

THE RANGE-TOPPING CAYENNE looked very similar to its less expensive siblings, but power-wise it was very different.

Under the bonnet was a 4.5-litre V8 engine that was fed by twin turbochargers. The engine had a maximum output of 450bhp – that was a whole 200bhp more than the entry-level Cayenne!

Performance was astonishing for an off-roader, with a 0-62mph time of just 5.6 seconds and a top speed of 165mph.

As standard, the car was equipped with a six-speed Tiptronic transmission that fed all four wheels, using Porsche Traction Management, that controlled the power the front and rear as required.

Also standard was air suspension that allowed the ride height to be adjusted to suit the conditions. Porsche Active Suspension Management adjusted the damper settings constantly to suit the road surface and manner of driving.

SPECIFICATION

Capacity: 4511cc

Compression ratio: 9.5:1

Maximum power: 450bhp at 6000rpm

Maximum torque: 620Nm at 2250-4750rpm

Brakes: Front: 350mm discs; rear: 330mm discs. Servo assisted with ABS

Wheels & tyres: Front: 18x8.0J with 255/55R18 tyres. Rear: 18x8.0J with 255/55R18 tyres (19- and 20-inch rims optional)

Length: 4786mm

Width: 1928mm

Weight: 2355kg

2004 **Carrera**

FOR MANY, THE 993 WAS THE BEST-looking 911 ever, so Porsche drew on that car's lines for the first new 911 of the 21st century. Code-named 997, the car's wings became more shapely and the body less slab-sided, while at the front the headlamps had an unashamed 993 influence. The indicators were housed in the front bumper; again, as per 993. However, there was more to the 997 than just this – Porsche claimed it to be 80 percent new compared to the outgoing model.

The 997 Carrera had essentially the same 3.6-litre engine as the 996, but it was fine-tuned to give an increased power output of 325bhp at 6800rpm (a modest 5bhp increase), while a new exhaust system brought back some of that traditional 911 soundtrack. The power went to the rear wheels only via a revised six-speed gearbox, while an automatic Tiptronic S was optional.

SPECIFICATION

Capacity: 3596cc
Compression ratio: 11.3:1
Maximum power: 325bhp at 6800rpm
Maximum torque: 370Nm at 4250rpm
Brakes: Front: 318mm discs; rear: 299mm discs. Servo assisted with ABS
Wheels & tyres: Front: 18x8J with 235/40ZR18 tyres. Rear: 18x10J with 265/40ZR18 tyres
Length: 4427mm
Width: 1808mm
Weight: 1395kg (coupé)

2005 **Carrera S**

THE CARRERA S WAS A MORE powerful version of the 997-model 911 and had a 3.8-litre engine that developed 355bhp – up 30bhp on the standard car.

Porsche Active Suspension Management (PASM), which was optional on the Carrera, was standard on the Carrera S. It allowed the driver to switch between a softer damper setting for everyday use that automatically firmed up during spirited cornering, and a Sports setting for serious driving on road or track.

The Carrera S had 19-inch wheels that housed larger 330mm ventilated brake discs with red-painted calipers. Porsche's ceramic brakes (with yellow calipers) were optional.

Inside, the Carrera S could be distinguished by its aluminium-coloured instruments. In other ways, it had the same interior as the 997-model Carrera.

SPECIFICATION

Capacity: 3824cc
Compression ratio: 11.8:1
Maximum power: 355bhp at 6800rpm
Maximum torque: 400Nm at 4250rpm
Brakes: Front: 330mm discs; rear: 330mm discs. Servo assisted with ABS
Suspension: Front: Lower wishbones and MacPherson struts with combined coil springs and dampers, plus anti-roll bar Rear: Multilink with combined coil springs and dampers, plus anti-roll bar
Wheels & tyres: Front: 19x8J with 235/35ZR19 tyres. Rear: 19x11J with 295/30ZR19 tyres
Length: 4427mm
Width: 1808mm
Weight: 1420kg (coupé)

2005 **Boxster**

FOR 2005, THE BOXSTER RECEIVED a major make-over. The front was treated to oval, 997-style lights and a new nose with large intakes. At the back, meanwhile, the wings became more shapely and there were new light clusters.

The interior was all-new, with a neater instrument binnacle, round air vents, and an angular centre console that was similar to that in the 997-model 911. The three-spoke steering wheel was also not unlike the 911 item.

The same 2.7-litre engine was retained, albeit tweaked by 12bhp to produce 240bhp. This gave a 0-62mph time of 6.2 seconds and a top speed of 159mph. Standard fare was a five-speed gearbox, while a six-speed manual was optional, as was Tiptronic.

Another new option was Porsche Active Suspension Management which allowed the suspension to be adjusted from a softer, comfortable ride, to a harder setting for sporty driving. Effectively giving two cars in one.

SPECIFICATION

Capacity: 2687cc
Compression ratio: 11.0:1
Maximum power: 240bhp at 6400rpm
Maximum torque: 270Nm at 4700-6000rpm
Brakes: Front: 304mm discs; rear: 299mm discs. Servo assisted with ABS
Wheels & tyres: Front: 17x6.5J with 205/55ZR17 tyres. Rear: 17x8J with 235/50ZR17 tyres
Length: 4329mm
Width: 1801mm
Weight: 1295kg

2005
Cayman S

IN 2005 PORSCHE LAUNCHED A new model. The Cayman S was priced between the Boxster and the 911 Carrera, and was claimed to offer a pure driving experience.

The car was, in fact, based on the Boxster and used essentially the same mid-engined platform.

However, it was powered by a 3.4-litre water-cooled flat-six engine that was based on the 911 unit and produced 295bhp.

The body was obviously Boxster-based but a fixed coupe roof gave the Cayman S the look of a mini 911.

Chapter 4

Things you didn't know about Porsche

1. In the 1950s, Porsche built tractors which, like the company's cars, used air-cooled engines (in two- and four-cylinder form). The lack of water cooling helped make the tractors very reliable and so liked by farmers in mainland Europe.

2. Porsche's famous badge has in its background the crest of the state of Baden-Wüttemberg with its curving stag horns. In the centre is the crest of the city of Stuggart with its rampant horse – the city began as a stud farm (the name derives from stud garden). The badge was designed by Ferry Porsche in 1952 and first appeared on cars the following year, although initially only on the steering wheel bosses. It first appeared on a bonnet of a 356 in 1957 has adorned Porsches ever since, with only minor updates.

LEFT The distinctive Porsche badge

3. Porsche designed and built a 1600cc aircraft engine in 1955. The horizontally opposed design of Porsche engines may be unusual in cars, but is more common in aeroplanes.

4. Film star James Dean was killed when his silver Porsche 550 Spyder, which he'd nicknamed 'Little Bastard' crashed in 1955. It was claimed that the wrecked car was cursed when its engine was fitted in another Porsche which subsequently also crashed badly. In the years following, the car was also responsible for a number of accidents when it fell or rolled onto mechanics.

5. 'Oh, Lord, won't you buy me a Mercedes Benz My friends all drive Porsches, I must make amends'. These lyrics from a Janis Joplin song are one of the most famous musical references to Porsche. The 100,000 Porsche to be built was a 1965 912 Targa, which was used by the German police.

6. The Porsche 928 won the title 'Car of the Year' in 1977 – the first sports car to do so.

OPPOSITE LEFT
The late film star
James Dean

LEFT Paul Newman
before the start of
Le Mans – 1979

7. The Porsche 914 was criticised for its boxy lines to such an extent that, in 1970, no less than four different car designers, including the Italian Giorgetto Giugiarp, proposed alternative body shapes for the entry-level Porsche. None was taken up by Porsche.

8. Starting in 1972, a number of lightweight Porsches have carried the 'RS' badge. RS stands for RennSport – which is German for motorsport.

9. Actor Paul Newman raced a Porsche 935 in the 1979 Le Mans 24-Hour race, and finished a very respectable second.

10. In 1975 Porsche created a Silver Anniversary 911, to celebrate 25 years of car production. 1063 examples of this silver-painted special were made and features included headlamp washers, uprated Blaupunkt radio, black trim, sports steering wheel and an uprated rear antiroll bar.

11. The 911 Turbo was available from 1976 with the distinctive Martini stripes as featured on Porsche racecars of the day. The so-called Martini Turbo was not, in fact, a model in its own right, but the stripes were simply an option.

12. Bullitt, the 1968 film, features a Porsche 356 as well as the more famous Ford Mustang and Dodge Charger.

13. The 911SC was built in the late 1970s and early 1970s. SC is said to be short for 'Super Carrera', although Porsche never marketed the car as such.

14. Porsche was involved in the design of the Russian Lada Samara car in the early 1980s.

15. The 911 Turbo SE of the 1980s cost almost double the price of the standard 911 Turbo when new.

16. Porsche was involved with the development of the cockpit design of the 1980 Airbus aeroplane.

17. A Porsche 928 gets crushed by a monster truck in the 1984 film Cannonball II.

18. Porsche claimed that only the roof panel of the 993-model 911 of 1993 was carried over unchanged from the previous model.

19. The Porsche 959 supercar was not designed to be sold in the US. However it is believed that a small number were shipped there and seized by customs. It is claimed that one of the cars is owned by Microsoft boss Bill Gates.

20. An episode of the US television show Friends was called 'The One With Joey's Porsche', in which Joey finds the keys to a Porsche.

21. 'A Learjet for the road' was how Porsche envisaged its stillborn four-door, feat-seater saloon car of the early 1990s. Codenamed 989, the car would have had 911-type lines but a front-mounted water-cooled V8 engine.

OPPOSITE LEFT Steve McQueen as featured in Bullitt

BELOW Joey 'Matt LeBlanc' (far right) and the cast of Friends

22. Some people refer the name of the early 1990s 964-model 911 Turbo as the '965'. This is incorrect – this type number was applied to a prototype high-tech 911 Turbo successor that shared much with the 959 supercar, and could have finally have been badged '969'.

23. The 1995 911 Turbo had 18-inch hollow-spoked wheels to save weight – a Porsche patented design.

24. The last-ever production air-cooled 911 was a Carrera 4S, built in 1998 and sold to US television star Jerry Seinfeld.

25. Although not an official model, a German dealer arranged for production of ten 911 Turbo Cabriolets for his customers in 1995. These had the previous generation 360bhp engine and rear-wheel-drive.

26. The name 'Boxster' is a combination of 'boxer' which refers to the engine design, and 'roadster' because the car is open-topped.

27. The 2001 GT2's rear wheels were 18-inches in diameter and no less than 12-inches wide with huge 315/30/ZR18 tyres. These were the widest wheels ever fitted to a production 911.

28. Although the all-new 996-model 911 Carrera was available from early 1998, Porsche continued to sell the old 993-model in Carrera 4 and Turbo forms during that year.

29. A Porsche 928 stars with Tom Cruise in the 1983 film Risky Business. Cruise borrows the car from his father without permission and gets into all sorts of trouble!

30. The 2004 997-model 911 had an aluminium bonnet, which Porsche said saved 3kg over the previous steel item.

31. Porsche refused to let its name be used in the PlayStation game, Grand Turismo, which is why the 911s in the game are branded Ruf – the name of a German tuning company.

32. Porsche developed the engine for the American Harley-Davidson Vrod motorcycle.

ABOVE Tom Cruise sat on a 928 in Risky Business

ABOVE Eddie Murphy in 48 Hours, alongside Nick Nolte

33. Eddie Murphy drove a Porsche 356 Speedster in the 1982 film 48 Hours. And in Beverly Hills Cop 3 he's seen in a metallic pink 968 Cabriolet.

34. The 1998 996 Carrera 4 was just 55kg heavier than the two-wheel-drive Carrera. By comparison, the first four-wheel-drive 911 – the 964-model of 1989 – was 100kg more than the equivalent Carrera 2.

35. The 911 Carrera 3.2 Speedster was the last 911 to be built at the original factory at Zuffenhausen. The all-new 964-model 911 was made at a new facility.

36. In 1988 875 special Anniversary Carreras were produced to mark 25 years of 911 production. They had no 'Carrera' badge on the rear, and inside were blue leather seats with Ferdinand Porsche's signature on the backs, and a commemorative plaque on the glovebox. At its maximum speed of 189mph air flows through the 996-model 911 Turbo's front-mounted radiators at 100 cubic feet per second.

37. The revised 996-model 911 of 2001 used slightly thinner glass in its windows then the original 996 in an effort to reduce weight.

38. The Porsche Boxster is built in Germany and by an independent contractor in Finland.

39. Porsche Design is a separate company that styles items as diverse as sunglasses, coffee makers, watches and golf clubs.

40. Over two-thirds of all Porsche ever built are still on the road today, making them more environmentally friendly than other more 'disposable' cars.

41. The Cayman S takes its name from a south American reptile, resembling a crocodile. The creature is small and nimble – just like the car!

BELOW Porsche Design watch

The pictures in this book were provided courtesy of the following:

GETTY IMAGES
101 Bayham Street, London NW1 0AG

With special thanks to:

PORSCHE WERKFOTO, GERMANY

NATIONAL MOTOR MUSEUM
Beaulieu, Brockenhurst, Hampshire SO42 7ZN

© NEILL BRUCE
Grange Cottage, Harts Lane, Burghclear, Newbury RG20 9JN

Design and artwork by Kevin Gardner
Based on an original design by Darren Roberts

Published by Green Umbrella Publishing

Series Editors Jules Gammond, Tim Exell, Vanessa Gardner

Written by Philip Raby